INVISIBLE ENEMIES

JEANETTE FARRELL

INVISIBLE ENEMIES

STORIES OF

INFECTIOUS DISEASE

FARRAR STRAUS GIROUX

NEW YORK

Copyright © 1998 by Jeanette Farrell
All rights reserved
Distributed in Canada by Douglas & McIntyre Ltd.
Printed in the United States of America
Designed by Filomena Tuosto
First edition, 1998
Third printing, 1999

Library of Congress Cataloging-in-Publication Data
Farrell, Jeanette.
    Invisible enemies : stories of infectious disease / Jeanette
Farrell. — 1st ed.
        p.   cm.
    Summary: The story of humankind's fight against seven major dangerous
diseases.
    ISBN 0-374-33637-7
    1. Communicable diseases—History—Juvenile literature.
[1. Communicable diseases—History.]   I. Title.
RA643.F37 1997
616.9'09—dc21   96-53247

Frontispiece:
The sufferings of Job, a woodcut by Hans Wechbelin from 1517

For my father, Charles J. Farrell, M.D.
1901–1977

ACKNOWLEDGMENTS

I feel tremendously grateful to the many people who have contributed to this book by reading the manuscript, answering my endless questions, tracking down illustrations, or giving me unfailing inspiration and encouragement. To mention only a few: Dr. James Whorton, Dr. James Plorde, and Dr. John Sherris all read the manuscript and contributed very valuable comments. Julia Rivera Elwood provided me with information regarding the Hansen's Disease Center in Carville, Louisiana. Dr. Steve Moseley battled tirelessly for illustrations on my behalf. My editor, Wesley Adams, had faith in this project and skillfully guided it into being. Elaine Chubb blessed my manuscript with her exquisite scrutiny. Filomena Tuosto worked magic with the book's design. Elisabeth Kallick Dyssegaard, ever wise and generous, showed me that I could tell these stories. I want to extend special thanks to an anonymous reader whose insight and comments greatly enriched this book. Finally, without David Sherman as muse, editor, and cook, for whom no task was too big or too small, this book would not have been written.

CONTENTS

All interest in disease and death is
only another expression of interest in life.
—Thomas Mann, *The Magic Mountain*

INTRODUCTION

ATTACK OF THE TINY GIANTS

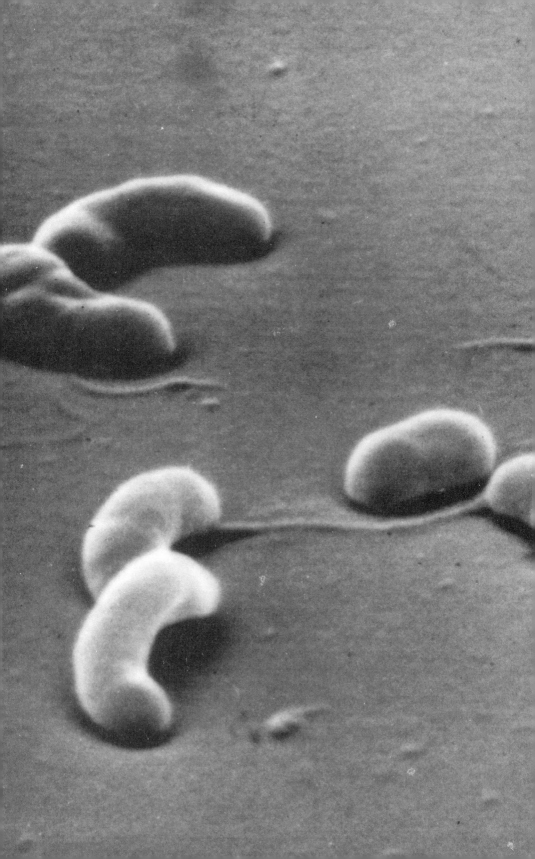

When George Washington first felt the soreness in his throat on that cold December afternoon in 1799, he must have known that even he, master of Mount Vernon, first President of the United States, conqueror of the British Army in the war for American independence, could be up against a foe he might not defeat. Despite nasty weather the day before, Washington had ridden his horse through the windblown rain, hail, and snow to oversee his farm. The next morning he felt the beginnings of a cold, and it was during the next night that he woke his wife to tell her he had grown chill and feverish. At first light his friend Dr. James Craik was called.

A concerned Dr. Craik called two other physicians, Dr. Elisha Dick of Alexandria, Virginia, and Dr. Gustavus Richard Brown of Port Tobacco, Maryland, assembling the finest in medical care to be had. Their course of treatment was to have George Washington inhale vinegar and water, gargle a mixture of vinegar and sage tea, undergo an enema, and take three doses of calomel and sev-

The bacterium that causes cholera seen through a scanning electron microscope at 29,000 times its actual size

eral more of tartar emetic. They raised blisters on Washington's skin, rubbed vinegar on his throat, and drained from his veins as much as two quarts of blood. By the middle of the day, Washington announced, "I find I am going, my breath cannot last long. I believed from the first that the disorder would prove fatal." By late afternoon, he told a doctor that he was "not afraid to go."

At eleven-thirty that night, December 14, 1799, George Washington was dead. His doctor reached up and stopped the hands of his bedroom clock.

George Washington, former President of the United States, got a sore throat and believed from the first that it could kill him. That assumption was understandable in 1799. But today, two hundred years later, we would not expect to die from a sore throat. In the two centuries since Washington's death, the way we live with infectious disease has completely changed: we have found the microbes that cause infections and we have learned how to kill many of them. The story of humankind's struggle with disease shows us both how far we have come and how much we still have to learn.

This book tells the stories of seven infectious diseases that have had a profound impact on human history, diseases that have caused great suffering, and that have brought forth our best and our worst traits as we have struggled to understand and control them. They are smallpox, leprosy, plague, tuberculosis, malaria, cholera, and AIDS. Infectious diseases are diseases caused by the invasion of the body by the tiny organisms we call germs. These organisms can pass from one body to another and so spread disease. Many diseases are not infectious—heart disease and most cancers, for instance—and are caused not by microorganisms but by other factors, such as poor diet or inherited problems.

All disease troubles us deeply because it stops us in our tracks. On most days, we go about our business not thinking about our body, merely using it to get where we want to go. But when we get sick we can think of nothing but our aching head or upset stomach. We feel at the mercy of forces beyond our control. Infectious diseases have another troubling aspect: sometimes the disease comes to us from another person. This can turn the fear of disease into fear of one another. It is in response to this fear that humans have been both incredibly brave and incredibly cruel.

It was in the 1500s that an Italian physician, Girolamo Fracastoro, suggested that disease was spread by invisible bodies. He called these tiny things *seminaria contagium,* or seeds of contagion. Fracastoro said that some of these tiny bodies passed from person to person when they touched, while others could linger on a shirt or a sheet and infect the next person who touched it. Still others needed no touch at all but could travel through the air. He proposed that these tiny, too-small-to-see things were the source of the great suffering of infectious disease. This was an idea that caught people's attention. It explained much of what people saw when they watched diseases spread. Infectious diseases like plague and smallpox that once struck in the sudden, widespread outbreaks known as epidemics clearly traveled from city to city and from household to household. But so much was still a mystery: when plague came to town, for instance, why did some people die while others did not? And could a person's life depend on nothing more than whether or not he or she touched a blanket that had tiny, nasty particles on it? And how could anyone prove the existence of things too small to see?

It was one hundred and thirty years later, in the late 1600s, that something remarkable happened: Antony van Leeuwenhoek found a way to see these tiny things. Leeuwenhoek lived in Delft, in the Netherlands. He was a draper by trade and also made hats, surveyed land, and kept the town-meeting house in order. In his spare time, Leeuwenhoek made magnifying lenses. The naked human eye cannot see things smaller than one tenth of a millimeter, but for hundreds of years people had known that by using a curved piece of glass one could magnify small things and make them easier to see. Leeuwenhoek managed to shape a piece of glass into a lens with such skill that he could use it to examine things that were smaller than anyone had ever seen.

In a letter dated October 9, 1676, he wrote of his experiments:

In the year 1675, about mid-September . . . I discovered living creatures in rain-water, which had stood but a few days in a new cask . . . This encouraged me to investigate this water closely, the more so since these [animals] were, to my eye, more than ten thousand times smaller than the [animal] . . . named the water-flea or water-louse, and which one can see living and moving in water with the unaided eye.

In the 1600s, when the fastest that news could spread was the speed of a galloping letter carrier's horse, it would have been possible that this draper in Delft would have made these great lenses and seen into this amazing world and no one would ever have known. Luckily for us, however, at that time there was a group of men interested in science who had formed the Royal Society of London. This society encouraged thinkers all across Europe to write to them with their ideas and discoveries so that they could publish and share them and build on one another's work. It was in his letters to the Royal Society that Leeuwenhoek told the world of the unimaginable creatures he saw when he looked in lake water, and seawater, and rainwater; on cheese, in vinegar, and in the scum scraped off his teeth; creatures that he found, in fact, just about everywhere he looked. For fifty years Leeuwenhoek wrote of his discoveries, and the world responded with amazement. Everyone who was anyone in Europe, from royalty to scientists, wanted to come and look through the microscope of the draper from Delft. And they were amazed by what they saw. In one letter, Leeuwenhoek wrote:

> *I have had several gentlewomen in my house, who were keen on seeing the little eels in vinegar: but some of 'em were so disgusted at the spectacle, that they vowed they'd ne'er use vinegar again. But what if one should tell such people in future that there are more animals living in the scum on the teeth in a man's mouth, than there are men in a whole kingdom? Especially in those who don't ever clean their teeth.*

Leeuwenhoek and the microscopists who followed him described the different types of creatures of this miniature world. There were the short straight skinny rods which they called bacilli, the tiny comma-like curves known as vibrios, the long thin tight coils called spirilla, and the chains of tiny beads named cocci. Some creatures were unable to move on their own and just drifted; others had tiny appendages that worked like oars to propel themselves along. Those that were long coils could move in a twirl as if they were a screw. Some slid along by oozing in one direction or another.

In time, scientists saw that there were two distinct types of these single-celled creatures. One type is small and simple. Its insides do not appear organized in any way. Hundreds can fit on the tip of a pin. Microbes of this type include the bacteria, some of which infect people. The other type is somewhat larger and much more complicated. Inside are some tiny structures rather like the organs in our body. Among these more complicated creatures are the protozoa, which when they infect people or other organisms are called parasites.

Another tiny infective agent, the virus, was even harder to find than Leeuwenhoek's creatures. Viruses are not even a cell; they are nothing but a blueprint for re-creating themselves tucked inside a protein envelope. All by itself a virus can do nothing, but when delivered to a cell where its message can be read, it can order the cell to do its bidding. Smallpox and AIDS are both caused by viruses. Viruses are so small that millions could fit on a pinhead. They could be made visible only after the invention in the twentieth century of a microscope that used electrons instead of light. In the 1930s scientists found ways to use beams of the tiny electrically charged particles called electrons to interact with very tiny objects in ways that allowed us to see their shapes.

But once humans could see the creatures in the scum on a tooth, for instance, questions remained: What did these tiny living creatures, the microbes, do, and where did they come from? Many people insisted that they simply developed from the stuff on our teeth itself. They thought that if you took the right ingredients and put them together, these little creatures would form, especially if things were beginning to rot. Let a piece of meat lie around for a few days, they said, and lo and behold, little white worms called maggots will appear on it. So it is, they said, with water that sits around, or the old bits of food that linger on our teeth. After some time, tiny creatures develop out of rotting stuff.

But others argued that since these little white worms on meat eventually develop into flies, they did not come from the rotting meat but from flies that came and laid their eggs in the meat. And the tiny creatures in the stuff on our teeth also came from somewhere else, perhaps from the food we ate or the air we breathed. Leeuwenhoek had seen tiny creatures just about everywhere, after all. No life develops from things that are not alive, these people argued, and these tiny creatures are simply the offspring of other tiny creatures.

This argument went on and on for hundreds of years until a few people did some clever experiments that convinced everyone

once and for all. The most important of these were the discoveries made by the French scientist Louis Pasteur in the nineteenth
century. Pasteur proved that microbes appeared in a solution only
after it was exposed to the microbe-filled air. Pasteur also established that one could make sure that there were no microbes in a
solution by heating it to a high enough temperature. At high tem-
peratures, all the microbes in a jar of water, say, would be killed.
If the jar was kept sealed, so no more microbes could get in, it
would remain sterile, or free of microbes.

Now it only remained to link the existence of these invisible
creatures to someone's sore throat—to prove that among the
swirling multitude of microbes that could be found in anyone's
mouth, most of them harmless, there was a certain one that
caused disease. This was accomplished by the German scientist
Robert Koch, a contemporary of Pasteur's. Koch was the first scientist to prove a particular tiny being caused a disease. In 1876 he
found the germ that caused anthrax, a disease largely of sheep,
cattle, and other animals. To do this, Koch had to discover how to
isolate one type of these creatures from all the others that happened to live in a sick person, grow this creature and this creature
alone in his laboratory, and then place this creature in an animal
and make it sick.

The efforts of Pasteur and Koch were to revolutionize our
understanding of infectious disease. While in 1799 the cause of
Washington's death was a mystery, by the end of the next century,
in a mere one hundred years, the microbes that caused diphtheria, tetanus, plague, botulism, cholera, tuberculosis, leprosy, typhoid fever, and malaria, as well as types of pneumonia, dysentery, and meningitis, had all been identified. Humans had come to
understand that we shared this earth with tiny giants which, however small, could take control of a human life. Now that the
disease-carrying microbes had been discovered, we began to find

ways to control them. This was not as easy as we might have hoped.

In this book, you will read about smallpox and leprosy, diseases that appear to have been more or less overcome either by or in spite of human efforts. You will read about malaria and tuberculosis, diseases that no longer trouble the wealthy of the world but continue to cause great suffering among millions. You will read of cholera and plague, which linger on despite our efforts. And, finally, you will read of a new disease, AIDS, which the best efforts of medicine cannot yet contain. With all that we have learned in the past two hundred years, George Washington probably would have lived through his sore throat, but the battle against disease is far from over.

The discovery and identification of these microbes answer definitively what causes many infectious diseases and have shown us how to fight some of them. But infectious disease remains frightening and mysterious: to say our lives have been completely changed just because we have been infected with a microbe is not a satisfying answer. We want to know, why me? Or if our sister or brother is sick, we want to know, why not me? And we want to know, why do the hands of our clock have to stop at the hour that they will? To that mystery we have no better answer than did Washington's physicians two hundred years ago.

SMALLPOX

OF SCARS, SCABS, ORPHANS,

AND SPOTTY COWS

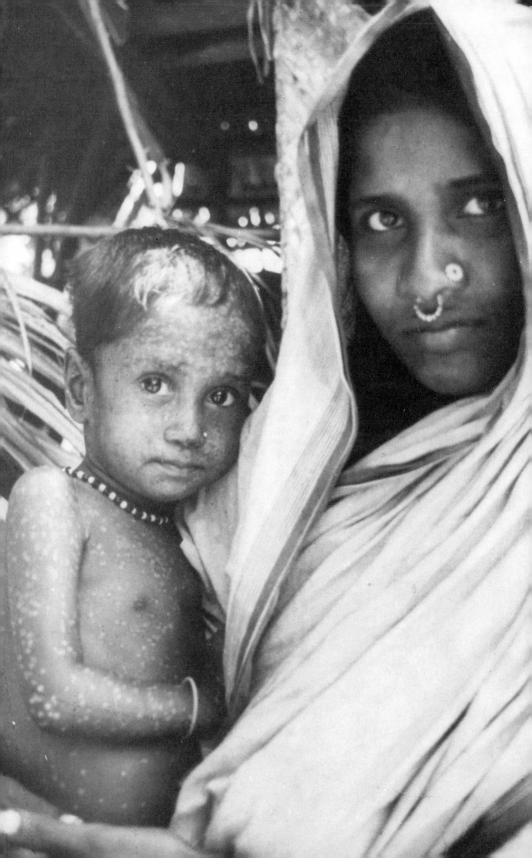

Pull up the sleeves of your mother or father, or an older friend. Pull them up high enough to expose their upper arms, and on one side you will probably find a dime-sized depression etched in the skin. One upper arm of most lucky people born after 1800 was marked with this little scar, proof of their protection against smallpox. Until 1800, there was no effective defense against this disease—a great French mathematician estimated smallpox killed, crippled, or disfigured one tenth of all humankind. And today, just two hundred years later, absolutely no one gets smallpox. If you were born after the mid-1970s, your arm has no scar of protection, because the disease has been wiped out. Officially, all the smallpox virus on the planet exists only in two laboratory deep freezers, one in Atlanta, and one in Moscow. On June 30, 1999, the World Health Organization (WHO), an agency of the United Nations responsible for monitoring and preventing the global spread of disease, plans to destroy these last samples and once and for all eliminate the virus that has killed millions of our number.

Two-year-old Rahima Banu of Bangladesh after she had recovered from what was to be the last case of smallpox in Asia, in November 1975

Of all the diseases humankind has fought, we have gained full control of no other. Not one. We may have beaten a disease back, at least in some parts of the planet, but no other disease have we managed to eradicate completely. Those dime-sized scars show how the killer smallpox was brought to its knees: they are the mark of vaccination. Smallpox survived only in the human body. Outside the body, on a page of a book, say, if it did not find its way into a human cell in a few weeks, smallpox perished. No other creature would do; no other animal could give the virus a home. This was the key to its defeat. Once every available human was protected by vaccination, smallpox perished. The smallpox stored in the laboratories in Atlanta and Moscow remains only because scientists preserved it to try to learn something from the disease that could help us treat a future scourge.

SCARS

Smallpox is a story told in scars. Smallpox took a face, smooth-skinned one day, then flushed with fever of unknown origin for four or five, until the telltale chicken-pox-like pustules, or pimples, began to rise, and then swell, burst, and dry. The highly contagious virus traveled easily; a drop of moisture exhaled from the lungs of an infected person teemed with a thousand more viruses than necessary to transmit the disease. The smallpox rash followed a pattern: pustules clustered on exposed places, on the face and the palms of the hands. In a bad case at its height, the eyes swelled shut. Death came when the body was overwhelmed by its fight with the virus: the body released so many powerful toxins in its struggle with the disease that sometimes victims were poisoned by their own chemical weapons. They slipped into shock and died. The lucky ones who survived could expect a face covered with shallow dishes, like the face of the moon, or a rain-spattered beach. The scars they could not hide marked survivors, so that people noticed how they never again caught the disease. The scars on their faces made it perfectly clear that people who once had smallpox and survived were now immune—they would never again get the disease—and people all over the world, hungry for that protection from death, began to think.

Lady Mary Wortley Montagu was renowned at the British court of the first years of the eighteenth century for her beauty and her wit, and after 1715 for her wit alone. The poets still wrote about her eyes; left lashless after the smallpox, they stood out brilliantly in her pockmarked face. But Lady Mary knew what she had

Lady Mary Wortley Montagu, in Turkish costume

been spared: two years before, smallpox had killed her only brother, the youngest of the family, when he was just twenty-one. Smallpox was to take the life of her best friend, and of her sister's son. And it nearly killed Lady Mary.

Upon her recovery, the scarred, twenty-six-year-old socialite did not know that, in infecting her, the wily smallpox that stole her beauty was sowing the seeds of its own destruction. Lady Mary, lashless and pockmarked, would soon travel to Turkey and discover that there, as in East Asia, and in Africa, and in India, when people had thought about the fact that those with pockmarked faces never again caught the disease, they had developed a way to give a minor case of smallpox that left the victim alive and discreetly scarred, and yet immune. Long before anyone even began to understand what it meant to be immune, Lady Mary simply saw that this practice, called inoculation, worked. Lady Mary would one day bring this practice back to England, and thus set the stage for an Englishman, Edward Jenner, in 1796, to develop vaccination and defeat smallpox.

In 1716 Lady Mary's husband became ambassador to the Ottoman Empire (Turkey). At that time, this was a most exotic destination for the British, months of travel away. On Wednesday, August 1, Lady Mary set off with her husband and their three-year-old son, Edward. It was a three days' sail for them just to reach Holland. From there they traveled by horse-drawn carriage overland through Cologne, Vienna, and Prague, with stops at all the appropriate palaces, taking nearly a year. Along the way Lady Mary wrote renowned letters about the wonders she experienced. She wrote of greenhouses being used in Germany to grow lemons, oranges, and pineapples even in the frigid winter; of Turkish baths where the women were shocked by the straps and rigid bone stays of the corset she wore under her dress, thinking her husband had locked her up in them. It was before they even reached their destination of the capital of Turkey, Constantinople, that Lady Mary wrote the following historic letter to a friend:

Adrianople, April 1, 1717

I am going to tell you a thing that I am sure will make you wish yourself here. The small-pox, so fatal, and so general amongst us, is here made entirely harmless by the invention of ingrafting, *which is the term they give it. There is a set of old women who make it their business to perform the operation every autumn, in the month of September, when the great heat is abated. People send to one another to know if any of their family has a mind to have the small-pox: they make parties for this purpose, and when they are met (commonly fifteen or sixteen together), the old woman comes with a nutshell full of the matter of the best sort of small-pox, and asks what veins you please to have opened. She immediately rips open that you offer to her with a large needle (which gives you no more pain than a common scratch), and puts into the vein as much venom as can lie upon the head of her needle, and after binds up the little wound with a hollow bit of shell; and in this manner opens four or five veins ... The children or young patients play together all the rest of the day, and are in perfect health to the eighth, then the fever begins to seize them, and they keep their beds two days, very seldom three. They have very rarely above twenty or thirty [pustules] in their faces, which never mark; and in eight days' time they are as well as before their illness ... Every year thousands undergo this operation: and the French ambassador says pleasantly, that they take the small-pox here by way of diversion, as they take the waters in other countries. There is no example of any one that has died in it; and you may believe I am very well satisfied of the safety of the experiment, since I intend to try it on my dear little son.*

I am patriot enough to take pains to bring this useful invention into fashion in England.

One year later, Lady Mary carried out her plan to have her son inoculated. She had just given birth to her second child, a daughter. It was spring. Smallpox, like the terrible diarrhea of dysentery and the fevers of typhoid, came with the heat. The face that stared back at Lady Mary from any mirror warned her not to rely upon her luck.

The doctor wrote of the inoculation experience:

The Ambassador's ingenious Lady, who had been at some Pains to satisfy her Curiosity in this Matter, and had made some useful Observations on the Practice, was so thoroughly convinced of the Safety of it, that She resolv'd to submit her only Son to it, a very hopeful Boy of about Six Years of Age; She first of all order'd me to find out a fit Subject to take the Matter from; and then sent for an old Greek Woman, who had practis'd this Way a great many Years: After a good deal of Trouble and Pains, I found a proper Subject, and then the good Woman went to work; but so awkwardly by the shaking of her Hand, and put the Child to so much Torture with her blunt and rusty Needle, that I pitied his Cries, who had ever been of such Spirit and Courage, that hardly any Thing of Pain could make him cry before; and therefore Inoculated the other Arm with my own Instrument, and with so little Pain to him, that he did not in the least complain of it.

Once the doctor had left, Lady Mary had only to wait, several days until the fever, and two days more for the rash. The pustules would probably develop large and angry around the inoculation scars, but few and far between on the rest of the body, and very few, Lady Mary could only hope, on his face.

In the meantime, until the pustules rose and filled and burst, and the scabs dried up and fell off, the boy was to keep to his room. The virus was breeding in his body, and any contact could be lethal for his tiny month-old baby sister or her un-inoculated nurse.

Lady Mary had brought smallpox into their home. In doing so, she spared herself the grief her sister had to bear five years later when her son, who had not been inoculated, despite Lady Mary's pleading, died of the disease. Lady Mary was later to write of those who refused to inoculate their children that they were "fools, who had rather be sick by the doctor's prescriptions, than in health in rebellion." No doctor had been able to keep Lady Mary from losing her beauty.

Inoculation was not a risk-free procedure, however. At the time that Lady Mary had smallpox rubbed into her son's arm, had he been the one out of fifty who died of the inoculation, she would have had to live with the knowledge that she gave him his death. But Lady Mary's son Edward lived. No one completely understands why inoculation caused only a mild case of the disease, but usually it did. About a hundred pustules appeared, some dotting Edward's face, but they crusted and fell off without leaving any scars. Only at the places of inoculation did he carry the shallow-scooped marks that would stamp him as free from fear of small-pox for life. Lady Mary wrote to her husband that "the boy was engrafted last Tuesday and is at this time singing and playing, and very impatient for his supper."

ORPHANS

England was lucky that it was Lady Mary Wortley Montagu who went to Turkey as the ambassador's wife, for she was brave and bold, wrote good letters, and was friends with Caroline, Princess of Wales. When Lady Mary returned to England with her healthy son as proof of inoculation, her story of the operation impressed Princess Caroline. One of the princess's three daughters had nearly died of smallpox, and she was desperate to spare the other two. It was not for the royal family to be guinea pigs, however. Princess Caroline had six condemned prisoners inoculated first. In the summer of 1721, volunteers were called for from among the condemned men at London's Newgate Prison. This was their choice: be infected with a deadly disease and win their freedom if they survived, or continue starving in the sunless prison until the day that they would be hung. Six lucky men took a chance, and with the many physicians and surgeons and apothecaries who cared for the court looking on, the very same doctor who had inoculated Lady Mary's son rubbed smallpox into cuts in their arms. Five of the prisoners came down with mild cases of the disease and recovered completely; the sixth, who had had smallpox before, did not become ill. All were allowed to go free.

This was impressive, but the princess wanted further proof, with younger people. Her solution: use orphans! In the spring of 1722 she called for the inoculation of the orphan children of St. James Parish. If these young bodies could survive the inoculation, she would allow the same for her daughters.

Unlike the prisoners, the orphans were not given a choice, even a bad one. They were the first of many orphans whose lives would be risked in the fight against smallpox. Orphans were plentiful in London in the eighteenth century: some were not actually orphaned but were left by their destitute parents on a church's doorstep because their parents were afraid they could not afford to feed them. Foundlings were sometimes named after the parish and the day of the week they were found: there may have been a Tuesday and a Wednesday St. James among those inoculated.

If the orphans had been killed by the princess's experiment, if this had been just some crank cure that failed miserably and faded into the past, we probably would not even know of the orphans' deaths. As it was, inoculation was to lead to vaccination, which was to lead to eradication, and these nameless orphans have gone down in history. The orphans survived, and that April the little princesses were inoculated.

Once Princess Caroline had her children inoculated, the procedure became the fashion. All those in high society wanted to have their children inoculated. So Lady Mary had not only proved "patriot enough" to bring life-saving inoculation to England but also, through her friendship with the princess, made it a common practice.

TWO SLAVES AND FOUR SONS

It took Lady Mary's bravery, witty letters, and healthy son; six condemned prisoners; all the orphan children of St. James Parish; and three princesses to finally get the British inoculating in the eighteenth century. Meanwhile, in India, China, and Africa, people had thought of ways to inoculate many years earlier: everything from snorting the scabs of smallpox patients up their nose (in China) to having door-to-door inoculation teams, complete with supplies of dried pus and holy water to moisten it (in India). By the time the British began inoculating, inoculation in its many forms had been practiced around the world for hundreds of years.

We do not know the full story of the worldwide history of inoculation, because in many places no written records were kept of its practice. In Africa, for instance, knowledge of inoculation was passed from generation to generation by word of mouth; it was not written down. We do know that just as inoculation came to England from Turkey, it came to America from Africa in the person of Onesimus, slave to the famous colonial clergyman Cotton

Inoculation in China, commonly known as "planting the flowers," involved blowing smallpox scabs up the nose

Mather. But all we know of what Onesimus knew about Africa's practice of inoculation is his owner Cotton Mather's written words.

Most probably the man who would later be given the slave name Onesimus was from the Gurumanche people, who lived in West Africa, although of his real home and even of the name of his tribe we have no clear record. Slave traders branded him with their mark, chained him by the ankle to another slave, and stuffed him and hundreds of others in the four-foot-high space between the decks of a slaving ship, to be carried as cargo. There, for the endless weeks of travel, Onesimus heard the moans of men dying from fever and dysentery, and watched as others chose to die, refusing to eat, until the slavers pried open their mouths to shove food down their throats. Somehow, Onesimus kept his mind and spirit alive. In surviving, he brought to the people that enslaved him the secret to saving thousands of lives.

This Gurumanche man was purchased for forty English pounds for Cotton Mather by Mather's congregation. He was a valued slave: Cotton Mather called Onesimus a "smile of heaven upon our family." When Mather asked if Onesimus had had smallpox—an important question, as an immune slave who could survive an epidemic was much more valuable—the slave gave the curious answer of yes and no. He showed Mather a round, dark scar on his arm, and explained that he had been given a small case of smallpox so that he would not get the full-blown disease.

This is how Cotton Mather recalled the incident (when he describes what the slaves told him, he imitates the pidgin English that they spoke):

Enquiring of my Negro-Man Onesimus, *who is a pretty Intelligent Fellow, Whether he ever had ye Small-Pox, he answered* Yes *and* No; *and then told me that he had undergone an Operation, which had given him something of ye Small-Pox, and would forever preserve him from it, adding, That it was often used among ye* Guaramantese, *and whoever had ye Courage to use it, was forever free from ye Fear of the Contagion. He described ye Operation to me, and showed me in his Arm ye Scar . . . I have since mett with a Considerable Number of these* Africans, *who all agree in one Story; That in their Countrey* grandy-many *dy of the* Small-Pox: *But now they Learn This Way: People take Juice of* Small-Pox; *and cutty-skin, and putt in a Drop; then by'nd by a little* sicky, sicky, *then very few little things like* Small-Pox; *and no body dy of it; and no body have* Small-pox *any more. Thus in* Africa, *where the poor creatures dy of the*

Small-Pox *like Rotten Sheep, A Merciful God has taught them an* Infallible Preservative. *Tis a* Common Practice, *and is Attended with a* Constant Success.

Cotton Mather was so impressed by what this slave told him that he recorded it in his letters, his diaries, and the book he wrote about medical practices. When he also read accounts of inoculation in Turkey, he resolved to use this practice to protect Bostonians from smallpox.

Mather soon had his chance: in mid-April of 1721 the smallpox epidemic that inspired the British princess to inoculate arrived in Boston harbor, carried aboard the ship *Seahorse* from the West Indies. It was to be the worst smallpox epidemic in eighteenth-century Boston. By July so many people were dying that the constant ringing of funeral bells drove the living to distraction and terrified the sick. The city ordered that only one bell could be tolled at a time, and then only at designated hours.

The fact that the last smallpox epidemic had been nineteen years before allowed this one to be so fierce: all those born in the intervening years had had no chance to be exposed to the disease and to become immune. The city was full of potential victims. The smallpox virus could spread by the millions in the air exhaled by the infected. Inhaling as little as one virus particle could be enough to cause disease. Despite the city's efforts to isolate the infected by hanging red flags at the doors of their houses so that the uninfected would know to stay away, six thousand Bostonians contracted smallpox. Those who could fled the town, leaving their businesses and homes boarded up; the half-empty town seemed full of death.

In the American colonies, as in England, the pioneers of inoculation experimented on their children. On June 24, as the epidemic began to gather force, Mather wrote to a friend of his, the doctor Zabdiel Boylston, to say that now was the time to try inoculation. It was a terrifying prospect to take the deadly disease into one's home. But in the streets the terror was just as great. Zabdiel's wife and other children had left the city, leaving only six-year-old Thomas with his father. On June 26, 1721, Boylston inoculated him, as well as his thirty-two-year-old slave Jack and Jack's two-and-a-half-year-old son.

Long before their pustules rose, before even night had fallen on the first day, news of the inoculations spread through Boston. The city was horrified: a doctor had infected his own son with a deadly disease! Around many an inn table, men seethed about what they would do with Dr. Boylston. Someone tarred the saddle of a horse mistakenly thought to be his. Boylston went into hiding for two weeks, while men threatened to hang him. But nevertheless, as his child and slaves healed, Boylston was convinced inoculation worked. The fever and pustules passed quickly, leaving nothing but the inoculation scars to show for them. The doctor continued to inoculate, demanding that the critics come and view the health of his patients.

Mather, however, while a brave promoter of the cause, found his heart weak when it came to his own son. In June, Samuel came home from college at Harvard terrified because his roommate had died of smallpox. Samuel had not yet had it and therefore was not immune. His father was tormented. On August 1, he wrote in his diary:

Full of Distress about Sammy; *He begs to have his life saved, by receiving the* Small-pox, *in the way of* Inoculation, *and if he should after all dy by receiving it in the common Way, how can I answer it? On the other Side, our People, who have Satan remarkably filling their Hearts and their Tongues, will go on with infinite Prejudices against me and my Ministry, if I suffer this Operation upon the child.*

Mather had reason to worry. Like Lady Mary's child, Mather's son had a one-in-fifty chance of dying from the inoculation, and, until his pustules healed, he could give the disease to anyone else who was not immune. That August, Mather finally chose to risk inoculation and more community ill will. Sammy survived inoculation, and the epidemic, and became the only one of Mather's sixteen children that was to live longer than his father.

Cotton Mather, like Zabdiel Boylston and Lady Mary Wortley Montagu before him, had gambled with and for his child's life and had won. But in the story of inoculation, there was also a brave person who feared to risk inoculating his child, and was still brave enough to admit to and advise others against the mistake he thought led to his son's death.

Benjamin Franklin was a very young man when Zabdiel Boylston began inoculating in Boston. In 1721 he was apprenticed at his brother James's newspaper, the *New England Courant*. It was in the pages of the *Courant* that James published such fierce criticisms of inoculation that Mather referred to them as the work of the devil.

Fifteen years later, however, as editor of his own newspaper in Philadelphia, *The Pennsylvania Gazette*, Benjamin Franklin promoted inoculation. Therefore, when his four-year-old son, Francis, died of smallpox, it was all over the city that it was inoculation that had killed him.

Hearing this, the mourning Franklin was filled with even more anguish. Not only had he failed to inoculate his son but now his example, misinterpreted, could lead others to make the same mistake. Again, he took to the pages of his newspaper, and bravely he wrote (referring to smallpox as distemper):

Understanding 'tis a current Report, that my Son Francis, who died lately of the Small Pox, had it by Inoculation: and being desired to satisfy the Publick in that Particular; inasmuch as some People are, by the Report . . . deter'd from having that Operation perform'd on their Children, I do hereby sincerely declare, that he was not inoculated, but receiv'd the Distemper in the common Way of Infection; And I suppose the Report could only arise from its being my known Opinion, that Inoculation was a sage and beneficial Practice; and from my having said among my Acquaintances, that I intended to have my Child inoculated, as soon as he should have recovered sufficient Strength from a Flux with which he had been long afflicted.

The flux Franklin speaks of was probably dysentery, which was a common affliction of children in those days. Presumably, he had postponed inoculating the boy until he was well, and then never had the chance.

With the help of Franklin's promotion, inoculation did catch on in Philadelphia as well as in the rest of the colonies. It was common to prepare for the practice by days of rest and special diet and then to remain isolated while the infection subsided. High society made this the occasion for a party, like the inoculation parties in Turkey, a chance to invite friends in for a week so they could all get a minor case of smallpox together. Here's an invitation to one such party, dated July 8, 1776:

Mr. Storer has invited Mrs. Martin to take the small-pox at his house: if Mrs. Wentworth desires to get rid of her fears in the same way we will accommodate her in the best way we can. I've several friends that I've invited, and none of them will be more welcome than Mrs. W.

As you might imagine, inoculation was not a party to which everyone was invited. All this elaborate preparation, plus time off work for isolation and rest, made it a luxury. As a result, mainly

In this French cartoon circa 1750, a young boy is distracted by a marionette, while an inoculator administers pus taken from a pustule on the arm of the lady at left

the rich were inoculated, and the poor, the slaves, and especially the Native Americans continued to die of smallpox at very high rates. It was not until an epidemic in 1764 in Boston that inoculation was for the first time made available to the poor anywhere in North America.

SMALLPOX AND THE NATIVE AMERICANS

Smallpox did not exist among the native peoples of North and South America until the Europeans came. As no Native American had ever had the disease before, no one was immune: when exposed to smallpox, nearly everyone caught the disease, and nearly half of those who caught it died. In some villages so few adults remained to hunt that others starved. Those who caught smallpox but survived found their faces terribly scarred. They had never seen anything like it before.

Meanwhile, the Europeans strode among them seemingly invulnerable to the disease that was wiping them out. Because smallpox was so widespread in Europe, a majority of the soldiers and settlers would have been exposed by adulthood. These strange pale men seemed godlike in their immunity.

The Europeans, both colonists and conquistadors, were not above being thankful for the disease that gave them the upper hand. As the native people saw their invaders' immunity as god-like, so the Europeans talked about the disease as being sent by God to pave the way for their conquest of these lands.

In South America and Mexico, when the Spanish conquistadors came into conflict with the powerful empires of the Incas and the Aztecs, it was the disease they unknowingly brought with them that laid the Indian warriors low more than the conquistadors' superior weapons.

When the conquistador Hernán Cortés attempted to take the great Aztec city of Tenochtitlán, his troops were overcome by the Aztec opposition and forced to retreat. But the conquistadors had left behind the smallpox virus in Tenochtitlán, and while Cortés and his men reorganized and prepared a renewed assault, smallpox made its way through the city, killing, blinding, and scarring the Aztecs, and leaving fear and disorganization in its wake. One of Cortés's followers was later to write: "When the Christians were exhausted from war, God saw fit to send the Indians smallpox." When Cortés launched a second assault, the people of the great city, weakened by the disease, fell to his handful of men. Smallpox is thought to have killed three and a half million native people in Mexico.

In the north, when the Pilgrims landed, they also brought with them smallpox and other scourges. Native Americans died in heaps, the settlers wrote, leaving villages nothing but piles of bones. Increase Mather, father of Cotton, wrote that this devastation rid the land of "pernicious creatures," making room for the growth of Christian communities. Up and down the East Coast, as settlers came in contact with them, the Native Americans were decimated by disease. In 1738 half of the Cherokee nation succumbed to smallpox. The horrified Native Americans believed they were being poisoned by the whites, and accused the English settlers of doing it deliberately. In some cases, they were right: the smallpox was so effective at killing them that some settlers found ways to infect native people with the disease, such as trading them blankets contaminated with smallpox scabs.

Smallpox's devastation of Native Americans was a horrible consequence of the meeting of two worlds and of a virus that proved so fatal to those who had never seen it.

A CUCKOO WATCHER AND SPOTTY COWS

Once inoculation was more broadly available, fewer people died from smallpox. But inoculation, because it involved giving someone a minor case of smallpox, was risky: the inoculated person could develop a deadly case and also could infect family, friends, and neighbors. The price of protection by inoculation was the continued spread of smallpox. No wonder that when an English country doctor named Edward Jenner found a way to become immune from smallpox without getting the disease, his praises were sung by kings.

The human immune system, the organization of cells and organs that protects a body against disease, is tremendously complicated, and immunologists—scientists who study this system—

are still a long way from understanding it. They observe what they can about the mysteries of immunity and then diligently investigate ways to make sense of these observations.

That is just what Jenner did. Jenner knew much less than any modern immunologist about the workings of the immune system. He had no idea that the key to improving inoculation was to inoculate with a harmless virus so similar to smallpox that it could stimulate immune defenses that could protect against the smallpox virus. He knew only what milkmaids knew, what farmers knew, what many other doctors and men in science also knew: that people who got a disease called cowpox were said to be immune from smallpox. But Jenner did the work to prove it.

Jenner was a doctor who left London, a hotbed of scientific thinking, to return to his beloved birthplace in the country, where he could spend his spare time wandering the fields studying the curiosities of nature. He had made an interesting discovery about cuckoos, who lay their eggs in other birds' nests. He observed tiny two- and three-day-old cuckoo hatchlings tossing their nestmates out of their rightful nest by using a special temporary depression in their back. One can only imagine the hours of nest-watching it took to witness this spectacle—hours not spent treating patients or reading about disease. When Jenner's paper on the cuckoo was presented to the Royal Society, there were many disbelievers. One critic said: "No bird in the creation could perform such an astonishing feat under such embarrassing circumstances. The young cuckoo cannot, by any means, support its own weight during the first day of its existence. Of course, then, it is utterly incapable of clambering, rump foremost, up the steep side of a hedge-sparrow's nest, with the additional weight of a young hedge-sparrow on its back."

It does seem pretty impossible, but perhaps it was this ability to observe and report even the most astonishing facts of nature that made Jenner just the person to observe and report that a disease of cows could save humans from smallpox, and to believe he had found a cure that would one day rid the world of this scourge.

Many a dairyman and milkmaid among Jenner's neighbors took it as fact that you did not get smallpox once you had had cowpox. Cowpox was a disease that caused sores on cows' udders. When milkers touched the teats, they could catch the mild disease themselves: sores developed on their milking fingers and they sometimes got a fever. Jenner himself observed that when he went on his rounds of inoculation, some people, who claimed to have had cowpox, did not get smallpox from the infected pus he slipped in their arms from a quill. Yet there were others, who also claimed to have had cowpox, whose arms swelled and on whom pustules rose as fat and red as anyone's. Jenner did not take this as proof against an old wives' tale, but he worried over it. He wanted to know more about this disease they called cowpox. He had to be patient: cowpox came and went with no foreseeable pattern. Some seasons, cows' udders for miles around would be spotty with pustules. Then the disease would vanish and not come back for another few years. But Jenner watched and waited as if cowpox were a baby cuckoo, and every poxy cow udder that he saw he studied, and noted, and even had an artist draw. Finally, he was certain: what they called cowpox was not one but several diseases, and only one of these gave immunity against smallpox. It occurred to him that if he could take this disease, the true cowpox, and inoculate with it, it could provide immunity to smallpox without infection.

Suddenly Jenner's morning bird-watching walks and his evening strolls were taut with anxious curiosity. He wanted to test his theory, but he had to wait for cowpox to return. His waiting

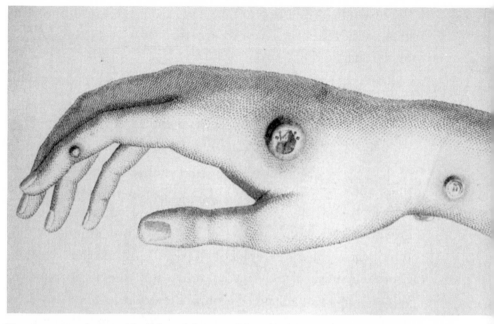

Drawing commissioned by Edward Jenner of the cowpox pustules on the arm of milkmaid Sarah Nelmes

finally paid off on May 14, 1796, when Sarah Nelmes, a milkmaid whose graceful hand has gone down in history, walked into his office. You can see in the drawing Jenner had made of Sarah Nelmes's arm that the pockmarks are where she would have brushed against the cow's udder as she milked it. Jenner took a quillful of pus from the milkmaid's arm and slipped it into a scratch made in the arm of a young boy named James Phipps. On his arm grew a pustule that resembled the pustules of Sarah Nelmes. Then it faded, leaving a simple, dime-sized scar.

On July 1, 1796, Jenner made the final test: he scratched young Phipps's same arm with smallpox. Nothing. Days passed. Still nothing. Once Phipps had been inoculated with cowpox, he could not get smallpox.

Jenner wrote: "The joy I felt at the prospect before me of being the instrument destined to take away from the world one of its greatest calamities . . . was so excessive that I sometimes found myself in a kind of reverie."

It was only after testing on child after child that Jenner, always cautious, published his results in a pamphlet. Inoculating with cowpox rather than smallpox became known as vaccination after the Latin word *vaccinus,* meaning "of a cow" (from *vacca,* "cow"). While those inoculated with smallpox developed dozens of pustules, could give their neighbors smallpox, and risked death for their immunity, those vaccinated developed one pustule, could give no one smallpox, rarely died, and were also immune. Within three years, Jenner's pamphlet had been translated into German, French, Spanish, Dutch, Italian, and Latin, and the practice of vaccination began to spread around the world.

Jenner went from country doctor to world savior. The empress of Russia sent him a diamond ring. In Berlin, Germany, people began to celebrate every May 14 as the anniversary of James Phipps's vaccination. Britain and France were engaged in the Napoleonic wars in Jenner's time, yet the ruthless French leader Napoleon released captured British soldiers when Jenner asked that they be pardoned. The President of the United States, Thomas Jefferson, wrote to Jenner: "It is owing to your discovery . . . that in the future the peoples of the world will learn about this disgusting smallpox disease only from ancient tradition." And he was so right: here we are.

TWO BOATLOADS OF ORPHANS

Early on, the biggest problem posed by vaccination was how to transport fresh, live cowpox to people. Cows were not always infected with cowpox, and even then they were not very portable and not everyone was within a day's horseback ride of an infected cow. People discovered that pus dried on threads could be carried, remoistened, and used, but after several weeks it lost its strength.

After smallpox struck his daughter in 1798, Charles IV of Spain was particularly eager to battle the disease. When Spain's colonies in America suffered an epidemic in 1802, Charles heeded their call for aid. But how to send Jenner's miracle across the Atlantic Ocean, at least a two-month sail away? The solution: use the arms of orphan boys.

Twenty-two orphans, aged three to nine years, were selected from two Spanish orphanages for the voyage. They were to be vaccinated two at a time every nine days. Thus there would always be a fresh pustule from which to make another vaccination. On the tiny ship, the *María Pita,* the boys only had room to sleep in one crowded pile. Lest the newly vaccinated infect the others before their time, the boys were watched day and night to keep them separate.

The expedition leader, Francisco Xavier Balmis, was a tremendously ambitious man and anxious to go down in history as the one who brought vaccination to the Spanish colonies of the New World. He was outraged when he landed in Puerto Rico and found vaccination had already arrived from the North American mainland, carried on threads, one year earlier. His outrage was so nasty and so evident that the Puerto Rican governor refused to give Balmis any new orphans to keep up the vaccination chain. Nevertheless, Balmis made it to Venezuela with one pox on one orphan intact and immediately began to vaccinate. Balmis and his deputy, Don José Salvany, brought vaccination to South America, but Mexico and Cuba proved to be disappointments for Balmis, as Cuba had already received vaccination material from Puerto Rico and then passed it on to Mexico. Still determined, Balmis set his sights yet higher: under new orders from Charles IV, he set sail from Acapulco, Mexico, with a fresh boatload of Mexican orphan boys and carried vaccination to the Philippines and China. So Balmis did go down in history, and the orphan boys, too, however nameless.

A PROLONGED GOODBYE

Even with this amazing cure that no one had ever imagined possible, smallpox was not quickly brought to its knees. You might guess that this would be the case because you may know that diseases, such as measles, that we can prevent with just a couple of shots still persist to kill children all over the planet. So it was that even as vaccination became required by law in Bavaria (1807), Denmark (1810), Norway (1811), Russia (1812), and Sweden (1816), smallpox epidemics continued to sweep across Europe. In 1837, 2,100 people died of smallpox in London. William Farr, in 1840, in the British medical journal *The Lancet*, compared the persistent preventable epidemics to throwing children off London Bridge, day after day.

Why did people still die from smallpox for so many years? To begin with, not everyone accepted that vaccination was a good thing. There were those who made their living as inoculators, for instance. When they realized vaccination would put them out of business, they began to campaign against it. And they were not alone. Some people objected to being given an "animal disease." Others thought stopping smallpox was standing in the way of God's will. Vaccination introduced a revolutionary idea: for the first time, humans could effectively prevent disease. Unable to fight most disease, people were used to accepting illness and death as they came. Some thought doing otherwise would be sinful. When countries finally tried to pass laws forcing people to be vaccinated, people protested that the laws violated their freedom of choice.

To promote vaccination, these illustrations compared the fate of two beauties, one vaccinated, the other not

Along with all these philosophical issues, there were practical problems with vaccination. The unsanitary method often used at first, arm-to-arm vaccination, frequently transmitted other diseases from person to person. Also, doctors had not yet determined how long after vaccination one stayed immune. Controversy among doctors over these last points fed anti-vaccination sentiment.

Even with compulsory vaccination laws in place, the Franco-Prussian War of the 1870s spread a devastating smallpox epidemic throughout Europe and from there to North and South America and Africa. It was not until the twentieth century, more than one hundred years after Jenner's triumph, that vaccination began to eliminate smallpox. Even with this slow start, by the end of World War II, in all of Europe, only Spain and Portugal still suffered from smallpox.

But the battle was far from over: when smallpox began to be controlled and people became less fearful of it, some stopped taking their children to be vaccinated. And for the poor it continued to be difficult to afford both the vaccine and the time and travel to have their children vaccinated. There was another problem in the hot regions of the world, which also happened to be the poorest countries: vaccine had to be kept cool to work. How could one transport—and keep fresh—live vaccine in tropical countries? Even if the vaccine did not go bad in days or weeks of travel on muddy roads, once it arrived at its destination there was no electricity to provide refrigeration for safe storage.

Despite all these difficulties, by the early fifties smallpox was eliminated in North America, Europe, Central America and Panama, and Japan, except when an occasional traveler brought a case from another country. In 1958 the Minister of Health of the Soviet Union, Viktor M. Zhdanov, declared his belief that smallpox could be eliminated from the entire world. The ease of ridding the Soviet Union of smallpox had impressed Zhdanov, and he remained frustrated that cases of smallpox still entered his country across the borders with Iran and Afghanistan. He saw that no one country would truly be free of smallpox until the disease was controlled in the entire world, and he believed that this audacious goal was possible.

In 1958 Zhdanov proposed that the World Health Assembly, the governing body of the WHO, undertake the eradication. In human history, the idea of completely eliminating a disease from the face of the earth was a new one, proposed only since the dramatic scientific advances of the late nineteenth century made humans bold enough to think we could control the life of the planet. So far, it had not worked well. Humans had already tried or were trying to rid the world of hookworm, yellow fever, malaria, yaws, and tuberculosis. In fact, the results of the attempt to eliminate malaria were so discouraging that a few years after Zhdanov boldly proposed eliminating smallpox, a great scientist, René Dubos, declared that eradication of any disease would one day be looked upon as the dream of fools.

Even now, with smallpox gone, it may be that René Dubos was right. Of all the diseases humans have come up against, only smallpox has fallen, and that conquest appears a series of great strokes of luck. In 1958, a century and a half after Jenner's discovery, there were still 77,555 cases of smallpox in the world, in sixty-three countries. If no fool had dreamed this impossible task possible, surely smallpox would still be here, and every child's arm would need Jenner's mark.

The eradication project had a mixed beginning. It was not until eight years later, in 1966, that countries had donated enough money to begin work in earnest. But scientists had given the project some valuable tools. One developed a simple way to freeze-dry vaccine so that it did not have to be refrigerated. Another developed a needle with a split tip that swiftly administered the correct amount of vaccine in each prick. One person could vaccinate more than one thousand a day with such needles. And vaccinators would need to work that fast to get the job done: the project directors estimated that 1,790,000,000 people would need to be vaccinated.

In every country where smallpox still existed, mobile vaccination teams of ten traveled, vaccinating nonstop for three weeks, and then taking one week off to rest. They found it was easier to coax people to come than to force them: in India, for instance, laws that fined those who did not vaccinate themselves or their children failed to get any more people to come and be vaccinated, and laws that forced people who had smallpox into isolation hospitals made people hide their sick relatives in fear. These discoveries were crucial: if such laws made people with smallpox avoid treatment, the laws would help spread the disease.

By 1973 smallpox remained in only five countries: Ethiopia, Bangladesh, India, Nepal, and Pakistan. But the struggle continued: there were 135,904 cases reported that year, more than in any of the previous fifteen years. The problem was to find all these cases of smallpox and to vaccinate everyone in contact with each case before the disease could spread. Even if the virus had already found its way into a contact's body, the vaccination could prevent the disease from developing fully.

The determined eradication teams went house to house looking for cases. In India alone, to do this required 120,000 trained workers. Going from village to village, they showed each householder pictures of a baby with smallpox. They asked if the person had seen anyone with such a disease, and they offered a reward. Eight tons of posters were hung, advertising on every tenth house a reward for anyone finding a case of smallpox.

The technique worked: by 1975, in all of Asia, only troubled, newly founded Bangladesh still had smallpox. In Bangladesh, the searches, the freeze-dried vaccine, and the split needles that could work so well were thwarted by floods, famine, and war. In October 1974 just ninety-one villages were infected with smallpox when the worst floods in twenty years struck. Rivers rose, fields and villages were swamped, the rice harvest was lost, and famine followed. People scattered across the land looking for food and shelter, and those from the infected villages mixed with the unexposed. By April 1975 the number of infected villages had risen to 1,280.

More than fourteen thousand health workers went to work on house-to-house searches. Jeeps, motorcycles, and motorboats to travel around the country were hurriedly bought or borrowed. Incredibly, by July, just three months later, only 131 infected villages remained. Workers began to refer to their endeavor as the final stage. Then, on August 15, Sheikh Mujibur Rahman, the first President of the new country, was assassinated. Civil war threatened. War would mean millions of people uprooted, the population of those 131 infected villages dispersed throughout the country, and the renewed spread of smallpox. The aid workers desperately kept up their work. They hid all their vehicles to avoid having them commandeered by rebel factions. Against all odds, peace seemed to be holding and, with it, smallpox continued to be driven back. By October 1975 only one person had the disease, Rahima Banu, a two-year-old girl. Three weeks later, Rahima had recovered and was no longer infectious, and smallpox was gone from Asia.

The only place in the world where smallpox now remained was also a place where civil disruption had hampered eradication attempts. After smallpox had been eliminated in Somalia, the disease persisted in neighboring Ethiopia. It was eventually eradicated there, but not before nomads roaming the vast desert that lay across the border between the two countries carried smallpox back into Somalia. By the time this was discovered, smallpox had spread through southern Somalia. The country declared an emergency, and in May 1977 WHO launched an all-out assault on the disease. One hundred and forty-one days later, on October 26, 1977, a twenty-three-year-old Somalian, Ali Maow Maalin, came down with what we hope will be the world's last case of naturally acquired smallpox.

This was not the last case of smallpox in the world, however. The disease was to strike again, for the last time, with a vengeance that seemed directed at human attempts to control it. Ten months

A smallpox eradication team in a Somali village in 1975

after Ali Maow Maalin recovered, Janet Parker, a forty-year-old photographer's assistant who worked at the medical school of the University of Birmingham in England, came down with a fever that developed into an intense rash. Thirteen days after her fever first appeared, smallpox was suspected and she was hospitalized. Doctors did what they could, but there was still—and remains to this day—no effective treatment for smallpox. On September 11 she died.

It happened that Mrs. Parker worked in rooms directly above the laboratory of Henry Bedson, a renowned expert on pox viruses who worked with live smallpox virus in his laboratory. Although it has never been determined exactly how Mrs. Parker became infected, air ducts from the pox virus laboratory ran up through the walls of Mrs. Parker's work rooms. On September 2 Henry Bedson attempted suicide, and he died five days later. So it was that smallpox, in taking its last life, also took the life of one of the scientists who had come to control it.

Mrs. Parker was not to be the last case of smallpox. Her parents had cared for her during her illness. On September 1 her father developed a fever, raising concern that he might be infected, but before that could be confirmed, he died of a heart attack. On September 7 her mother became ill with smallpox. She was to recover; her case is the last instance of smallpox infection that the world has known.

IS THIS THE END?

Smallpox is the one disease we have managed to eliminate and perhaps the only disease we will ever be rid of. This feat has been one of luck and opportunity: the disease eradicated was one that infected only humans, making it easier to control; that showed its infection through a very visible rash; and that left stamped on the faces of its victims the clue that led to an understanding of immunity.

Some people think we have pushed our luck by keeping smallpox alive in two laboratories. What if an accidental leak were to occur, like the one that killed Janet Parker in England? The further we get from the days of smallpox, the more people there are who are not vaccinated: if there were an accidental leak, millions of unvaccinated young people could catch the disease and spread it. Even worse than that, what if a terrorist were to break in and steal the virus and then hold the world hostage, threatening to unleash this deadly germ? And it is possible that the smallpox virus may be part of biological weapons arsenals in unknown locations around the world. (In case of emergency, WHO has enough stored vaccine and split-tip needles to vaccinate 300 million people, and 22 individual countries have their own stores as well.)

Yet other people think we are pushing our luck to kill the virus. This is a disease we know how to conquer; it might therefore give us clues to conquering a new disease, one we do not yet even know of, that lies in wait to claim the lives of our children. Future generations might have questions to ask of this virus. Smallpox, however vile, is a part of the web of beings that makes up life on earth. Is it right for us to decide to knowingly exterminate another species? If we kill smallpox, we can never go back.

We may never again face this bittersweet choice. In the years since eradication, René Dubos's words about foolish dreamers have only begun to ring more true. A new deadly virus, HIV, has emerged for which we have no cure, and old diseases we thought we had controlled, such as tuberculosis, have made a comeback. And the best efforts of eradication teams cannot prevent the illicit preservation of "eradicated diseases" for biological weapons: a dangerous disease is all the more deadly once no one is naturally infected. The short moment in human history when we were bold enough to attempt eradication may already be in the past.

LEPROSY

MISNAMED, MISUNDERSTOOD

Hansen's disease, commonly called leprosy, is one of the least contagious of all infectious diseases. This disease, whose victims are considered "untouchables" and who have been outcast by societies for centuries, is very difficult for one person to pass on to another. How difficult? More than 90 percent of the people in the world could not get leprosy if they tried, and the rest would probably have to live with a leprosy patient for years in order to get it. Every disease in this book is deadlier than leprosy and more contagious, yet it is "leper" that has come to mean anyone who is outcast. That is why, when their voice was finally heard, people with leprosy said to the world: We don't want this name.

People with leprosy prefer the name Hansen's disease, after G. H. Armauer Hansen, the discoverer of the germ. The germ, a bacillus that Hansen named *Mycobacterium leprae,* has strange habits: it seeks out the coldest places it can find in the human body and grows there very, very slowly. But most of the suffering of people infected with *M. leprae* has been caused not by the bac-

Woman with leprosy ringing a warning bell, from a fourteenth-century English manuscript

terium but rather by fellow human beings. Today, when the disease can be treated and cured, the big barrier to its defeat remains the mark of shame associated with the disease. Until the curse is lifted, those suffering from the disease may not be willing to come forward even to be cured.

WHAT'S IN A NAME?

Stanley Stein was twenty-one when a doctor first noticed a reddish, swollen patch on his wrist. The year was 1920; the place, San Antonio, Texas. Stein was working as a pharmacist. The doctor saw the patch as Stein stretched his arm over the counter to hand out a prescription. During the few weeks while the doctor futilely tried radium treatment—strapping radioactive material to Stein's wrist to try to eliminate the patch—it never crossed Stein's mind that this tiny spot foretold his future, that ten and a half years later he would lose everything he knew of life, even his name. His name at the time was not in fact Stanley Stein; that was the name he would take when he entered the leprosarium in Carville, Louisiana. Like other patients, to keep his family from embarrassment he left his old life behind at the door. The man his parents named Sidney Levyson became Stanley Stein.

But Stanley Stein and others at Carville refused to become what the world said they were. When he first heard his doctor say, "You have leprosy," Stein thought of the characters in the novel *Ben-Hur* being chased out of the city by a mob screaming "Unclean!" He searched over his life for what sin he could have committed to bring this disease upon him. But in time, he was to revolt against these thoughts. Although Sidney Levyson might change his name to protect his family from stupidity, Stanley Stein was going to reject the name of leper.

The man who became Stanley Stein had one bit of luck: his first doctor understood that leprosy was just a disease, and he told

Stein to go on living normally. So Stanley Stein opened his own pharmacy, fell in love, and contemplated marriage. Although the love affair did not work out, it had nothing to do with leprosy: his only symptoms were the patch on his wrist and a reddish brown mark on his left knee. He kept his diagnosis a secret.

For nearly ten years, his luck held. Then patches began to appear on his face, unfortunately at about the same time that his wise doctor died. Unable to admit to his friends and colleagues that he had leprosy, Stein became so ashamed of his appearance that he no longer went out in public. Finally he decided he needed to leave town, to find a place where no one knew him, and seek treatment.

With his mother accompanying him, Stein journeyed all the way from Texas to New York City, where he could feel anonymous. A family friend had given him the name of one of the best dermatologists in town. When Stein sought this skin specialist out, however, he discovered a man with no heart and little understanding. After examining Stein so roughly that one of his skin patches, or lesions, began to bleed, the doctor brusquely told him that New York laws forbade the treatment of leprosy patients with open wounds, and insisted that the place for him was inside the national hospital for leprosy patients in Carville, Louisiana. When Stanley Stein left to consult another doctor, the first doctor sent the health department after him. He even notified the hotel where Stein was staying of his condition, and Stein had to pay for the sheets he slept on because the doctor told the hotel owner to burn them. So, like so many before him, for no other reason than that society didn't want to live with him, Stanley Stein found himself in Carville.

But Carville was one of the few places where leprosy was being treated like a disease rather than a curse. It was looked upon as a natural problem, a problem to solve. This approach made the symptoms much easier to endure, and it also made a cure possible. It was at Carville that drugs would be discovered that were able to attack the leprosy bacillus. Carville's patients would be the first in the world to take them.

The first patients to arrive at Carville came there in 1894, traveling up the Mississippi from New Orleans by barge under cover of night. Led by a doctor and a newspaper reporter, a group from New Orleans decided they would no longer tolerate sending their fellow humans to live in the horrors of the old pesthouse where the city put people with leprosy and other contagious diseases. With the help of a local sheriff, they leased an abandoned plantation up the Mississippi River, south of Baton Rouge. Every step was a fight: it was even hard to find a wagon owner who would agree to transport patients from the pesthouse to the riverside. But finally, on the night of November 30, 1894, five men and two women made their way up the river on the barge, along with crates of food, their few belongings, and donated beds. When they disembarked at Indian Camp, as the old plantation was known, they found a crumbling, columned mansion that was being converted into their new home.

By the time Stanley Stein arrived in 1931, Carville consisted of the columned mansion, now restored to its former glory, surrounded by giant spreading live oaks draped with moss, a network of dormitories connected by covered and screened walkways, a baseball diamond, tennis courts, and a nine-hole golf course. More than 360 patients called it home. Since 1921 Carville had been run by the federal government as the national center for treatment of and research into leprosy. But what Stanley Stein saw when he drove through the entrance was the high metal fence topped with three strands of barbed wire and the guards at the gates. For all its comforts, the leprosarium was also a place designed to isolate leprosy patients. It was located at the end of a long, poorly kept dirt road; patients needed permission to leave. There was no telephone, and no post office, and outgoing mail was heat-treated to sterilize it. Patients were not allowed to vote and were forbidden by law to ride on public transportation. To visit some states, patients needed the approval of the state health authorities at their destination.

At Carville, one of the first fellow patients to visit Stein told him he brought to mind a former patient, also an intelligent man, who had committed suicide. Stein was left wondering what would befall him here in this place where he saw no hope.

FEELING NO PAIN

You probably wonder what someone with leprosy looks like. What kind of face could inspire so much fear? On his first day at Carville, Stanley Stein was afraid to go to dinner for fear of the deformed monsters he might have to stare at across the table. But

The National Hansen's Disease Center, on the banks of the Mississippi River, in Carville, Louisiana

when hunger and the breakfast bell drew him to the dining room the following morning, he found in fact a normal-looking crowd ranging from the beautiful to the homely. If nothing else, Carville was a place where leprosy patients could learn to accept their disease by learning how to separate fact from fiction. They learned that leprosy, which they often called simply "it," took many forms when it infected humans.

The shape the disease takes depends on a person's ability to fight the germ off. Most people win outright in their battle with the bacterium and never develop any sign of the disease. Others get a couple of swollen reddish patches, where their immune system is battling the invasion. These trouble them for a few months and then disappear once the bacterium is defeated. In still others, if left untreated, the disease does not recede: in some cases the germs nestle into the skin of the forehead, chin, and earlobes, causing them to swell, and then to furrow, gradually distorting the look of the face. If the bacilli move into the hair follicles, patients may lose their eyebrows and eyelashes, which adds to the strangeness of their appearance. In rare cases, leprosy left untreated for too long can invade the cartilage of the nose and cause the nose to cave in.

If leprosy does overcome the immune system, the slow-growing bug invades not only the skin but also the nerves, and that is where it does its meanest work. Giving little notice of its presence, the bug moves into the nerves and interferes with their function. Fingers, hands, toes, and feet gradually go numb; they can no longer feel any sensation. Meanwhile, the persons so infected, as they go about their daily life, do not realize that the loyal watchman pain has left them. When they pick up a hot pot, they don't realize that it is hot and keep holding it while it burns their hand. When a stone finds its way into their shoe, they keep walking, oblivious to the stone working its way into their foot; it could go as deep as the

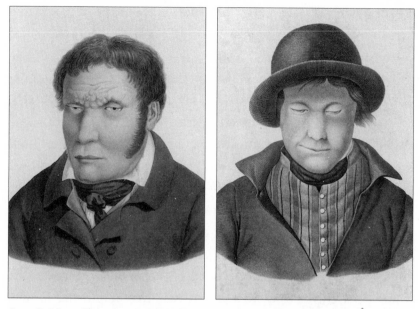

An artist for a French scientific expedition to Iceland in 1835–36 depicted the symptoms of two men suffering from leprosy: *M. leprae* has raised nodules on the forehead of the one and caused blindness and facial paralysis in the other

bone and they would not feel it. We are not used to being troubled by an absence of pain. Usually pain is something we try to avoid. But the stubbed hands and feet of people with advanced, untreated leprosy can remind us how valuable pain can be. Contrary to popular belief, their fingers and toes have not fallen off. Rather, because they felt no pain, they were injured again and again until the repeated wounds destroyed the flesh altogether.

In the outside world, leprosy patients who learned that the reality of the disease was much different from its myth—that fingers and hands did not fall off, that faces did not become monstrous —could not inform people of their misconceptions. Because patients were hiding their disease, they had to listen in silence to people's wrong-headed notions and cruel jokes. But within Carville, where "it" was the norm, the jokes were turned around. Stein wrote of one patient with a prosthetic leg who loved to alarm visitors by dropping his fake leg in front of them and screaming, "Oh! My leg just fell off!" to the visitors' horrified astonishment.

Leprosy is very picky. Of all the nerves in the body, leprosy invades only a particular few. In some it affects the nerve that tells the eyelid to shut—unprotected, the eye goes blind. In others it disables the nerve to the muscle that lifts the foot, so the foot flops from the ankle with each step. All the nerves it infects are those you can live without: with numb hands, numb feet, flopping feet, even blind eyes, you can go on living. No doubt this is part of leprosy's success: it is not deadly. It does not invade nerves that control essential life functions, so victims can remain alive to spread the slow-moving disease to others. This also means that leprosy patients have lived long lives as outcasts. Even after drugs to treat the disease were discovered in the 1940s, no one knew why the germ was so finicky or precisely how it spread. Scientists had, strangely, left the mysteries of leprosy largely untouched and these questions unanswered.

A TWO-THOUSAND-YEAR-OLD MISTAKE

After an initial depression, Stanley Stein realized that he wanted to be engaged with life whether he was in a leprosy hospital or not. Eventually he started a newspaper. His newspaper, *The Star*, became something unique: a way for the voice of leprosy patients to be heard. Over the years, *The Star* was to achieve a circulation of 45,000 people all over the world and to expand from its early days of running accounts of Carville social events and the patient cafeteria Thanksgiving Day menu to providing the latest news in leprosy research. It was in the pages of *The Star* that Stanley Stein began his campaign against the name leprosy.

Leprosy, it seems, was the wrong name to begin with. The word comes from the ancient Greek word *lepra,* which the Greek physician Hippocrates used to refer to a blotchy condition of the skin with none of the symptoms of nerve damage that today would make us think it was Hansen's disease. When the writings of the Old Testament were translated into Greek, about in the third century B.C., a Hebrew word, *tsara'ath,* which meant "unholy" or "unblessed," was translated by the Greek word *lepra. Tsara'ath* had been used to describe both people with strange-looking skin and buildings that had become spiritually contaminated in some way. What was *tsara'ath* could be cleansed only by religious ritual. Now the medical term *lepra* came to describe a condition that was originally religious, and the confusion grew. In time, this word came to describe those who suffered from the infection we now know as Hansen's disease, and along with the name came the meaning of ritual uncleanliness.

In Europe, from the time of the Crusades (A.D. 1095–1272) until the great plague epidemic of the fourteenth century, leprosy was widespread, for reasons that are mysterious, infecting more Europeans in those few hundred years than at any other time. Europeans considered leprosy to be a curse of sinners. When it was discovered someone had leprosy, the sufferer was often taken to the church, where a black cloth tent was erected before the altar under which the infected person knelt while a burial mass was said over him or her. Then the person was taken to a leper house, where the priest, as if he were throwing dirt on a grave, would throw dirt at the leper and say, "Be dead to the world and again living to God." People with leprosy had to wear special clothes or badges marking them as unclean; they had to carry a bell or strike together two sticks to warn people of their approach. They could not bathe in the village stream. They could not walk on narrow paths where someone might brush against them in passing. They could not speak above a whisper, so as not to blow their breath upon others. In some regions they were ordered never to touch a child. In others they were not allowed in the markets; in still others, not even in the town. During the reigns of Henry II of England (1154–1189) and Philip V of France (1285–1314) lepers were burned at the stake, and during the reign of Henry's great-grandson Edward I (1272–1327) they were buried alive.

But gradually something occurred to throw the status of leprosy into question. When at the end of the eleventh century the first crusaders began returning from their mission to reclaim the Holy Land from the Muslims, they were greeted as God's warriors. It so happened that leprosy was prevalent in the Holy Land, and some crusaders, while on their campaigns, had picked up the disease. When they began to show the unmistakable signs of leprosy, Europe was faced with a conundrum. For Christians, the warriors were doing divine work, saving souls by spreading Christianity any way they could, including by the sword. So how could these holy warriors, men especially blessed, suffer the disease of sinners?

The Church answered this riddle by finding a whole new aspect to leprosy in the Bible. Church leaders singled out the Old Testament verse Isaiah 53:4: "Surely he hath borne our infirmities and carried our sorrows; and we have thought him as it were a leper, and as one struck by God and afflicted." They declared that this verse was a prophecy that Jesus Christ would contract leprosy and thus the disease would become a holy disease. Some interpreted this to mean Christ had in fact contracted leprosy. Given this new twist, it became something of an honor to be infected with leprosy, to share the disease of the Saviour. It became an even greater good to be charitable to people stricken with Christ's disease. In fact, some people went to the opposite extreme: lepers, who had been thrown from their homes, who had been made to walk the streets ringing a warning bell, now to some became the objects of strange attraction. Those seeking to prove their piety established missions to the lepers, or went even further: the story is told that young King David I of Scotland, whose sister had married the King of England, found his sister one evening with a group of lepers in her chamber. There she was washing and kissing their feet with devotion. Aghast, David asked her what she thought she was doing and said that the King, her husband, would never kiss her again if he knew where her lips had been. She replied, "Who does not know that the feet of an Eternal King are to be preferred to the lips of a mortal king?" Across Europe, the pious took to kissing lepers, or climbing into their baths, or sharing their food, to prove their devotion.

While it may be better to have your feet kissed than to be buried alive, leprosy was still being treated as something religious, not as a disease. Why leprosy stimulates such a reaction remains a mystery. Why was leprosy out of all diseases marked as a curse? Even after men began to examine other diseases with a scientific eye and to explore their mysteries as puzzles to be solved, they left leprosy largely unexamined for years and years.

It was not just the biblical name that gave leprosy a bad reputation. In other cultures speaking other languages and reading other holy books, the same stigma arose. In the Japanese religion Shintoism, the word for leprosy is the word for sin. In India, leprosy was also considered a sign of sin. To explain these prejudices, we could say that it is because leprosy can show itself on the face and hands, leaving a permanent mark, that people reacted to it so. But we have read of smallpox, with its horrible pustules and scars, and smallpox was not considered a curse. Perhaps because leprosy struck more selectively, people could afford to hate those who had

the disease, as there would not be too many people to discriminate against. Or perhaps there is something about prejudice that can never be explained.

TWO INDOMITABLE NORWEGIANS

To make a difficult situation even worse, when people did begin to look at leprosy as a physical phenomenon that they could explore, they found the disease resisted all their attempts to study it. It took a scientist with a very personal experience of the physical realities of disease to change the way people saw leprosy.

Daniel Cornelius Danielssen was born in 1817 in Bergen, Norway, an unusually unhealthy city that was full of disease. Danielssen began his career at thirteen as an apprentice to an apothecary, but four years later this work was rudely interrupted when he developed tuberculosis of the hip. Tuberculosis, which is caused by a germ very similar to the one that causes leprosy, was more common than leprosy in most of Europe in those days. Some in fact believe that the easier-to-spread tuberculosis drove leprosy out of Europe after the Middle Ages by infecting many people with a similar germ and thereby rendering them immune to leprosy. However, for reasons that are not completely clear, in Bergen leprosy remained especially prevalent. But Danielssen got tuberculosis, and by infecting Danielssen, tuberculosis was to strike a great blow against its cousin leprosy.

While Danielssen lay in bed for a year and a half, struggling to overcome the disease in his hip, he began to study medicine. By the time he was twenty, shortly after his recovery, he passed his medical examinations and embarked on his new career. He de-

At an annual banquet held for leprosy patients in Nuremberg, Germany, patients had to earn their supper: they were examined, preached to, and required to make their confession and receive Holy Communion before they could sit down to eat

cided to observe exactly what the disease called leprosy did to the body. At that time, people who had all sorts of skin conditions, even comparatively mild ones such as psoriasis, were being diagnosed with leprosy and sent to homes for leprosy patients, where, over the years, they could actually get leprosy. Along with a skin doctor named Carl Wilhelm Boeck, Danielssen published a book that described not only the various types of leprosy but also, with careful explanation and illustration, the difference between leprosy and other skin diseases with which it had formerly been confused.

By making these observations and publishing them, Danielssen and Boeck started scientific minds all over Europe thinking about this illness not as a curse but as a disease. Danielssen went on to explore further what could cause leprosy. This is where leprosy led him off course.

Leprosy develops only in people whose immune systems cannot overcome it, and it appears that the ability to resist the disease runs in families. Therefore, in a study of who got the disease, a researcher would find that some families had a history of leprosy. Danielssen observed that leprosy showed up in the same families every other generation. He thought that this suggested leprosy was not contagious at all but was an inherited disease.

Danielssen decided to take a bold step. To try to prove that leprosy was not contagious, he began to inject himself with bits of tissue from leprosy patients to see what happened. Four of his assistants also offered themselves for these risky experiments. They would take a knife, nick the lesion of a patient, and draw the material into a syringe to inject it into their arms. As Danielssen had predicted, they did not develop the disease. He concluded that this meant that leprosy was inherited, not contagious. Danielssen was the foremost authority in the world on leprosy, and he had risked his health in a bold experiment that seemed to prove his point. All the same, he was wrong.

But Danielssen had brought to leprosy the light of scientific scrutiny: his conclusions about leprosy would not be believed unless they were supported by the observations and experiments of others. Scientific scrutiny would eventually lead to the recognition of his mistake. In 1841, in Danielssen's own hometown, Gerhard Henrik Armauer Hansen was born, the man who would become Danielssen's protégé, marry Danielssen's daughter, and challenge the truth of his life's work.

In his memoirs, Hansen describes the time when his family got their first kerosene lamp. Before that, their long Nordic winter nights were lit only by the small flickerings of candles. But the kerosene lamp "made a fabulous impression—a porcelain holder with beautiful painted flowers which, when lit, bathed the whole living room in brightness." During Hansen's lifetime, the observations scientists made about disease would throw ever wider circles of light upon the natural world, and change the way humans thought about life. In 1870, when twenty-eight-year-old Hansen had just begun his career, he was given the opportunity to go to Germany to study. He read of Charles Darwin's theory of evolution. "It began in an ordinary enough fashion with my walking into a bookstore, but when I came upon a copy of *On the Origin of Species* fate was at my elbow. Never had I read anything like it. The whole world stood out in an entirely different light than I had known." It was not just the theory that Darwin described which astounded Hansen, and the fact that Darwin had come up with an entirely new way of looking at the world, but it was also the way Darwin came to his conclusions. Through reading Darwin's works, Hansen wrote, he "reached the heart of scientific research and reasoning: to set aside every preconceived opinion and to diagnose from every approach that might have bearing on an ultimate solution. Nothing I had previously encountered had so fertilized my thought and my work. My goal had become that of researching as open-mindedly and honestly as Darwin had, to be as thorough and, at the same time, as cautious as he in arriving at my conclusions."

Hansen became convinced that leprosy was not hereditary at all but contagious and caused by a microorganism. When he returned to Norway, he still had the utmost respect for his mentor, Danielssen, but he thought that Danielssen was wrong, and Hansen began to determine how he might go about proving it.

For more than a year, whenever he had any spare time, Hansen would take a sample of tissue from a leprosy patient and study it under the microscope. What he was looking for he could barely describe himself. But Hansen steadily persisted in scrutinizing his samples, day after day, looking for something that he could not imagine but that he believed just had to be there. One day, February 28, 1873, he looked through his microscope and saw a collection of little sticklike things in one of his samples. He could not believe his eyes. He thought he had better make certain, by looking at yet more samples from other patients. Over the next few weeks, now knowing what he was looking for, he saw the little sticks again and again.

Hansen was certain that a tiny creature existed in the tissues of people with leprosy, and that it was the cause of the disease. But in order to prove this to others, Hansen had to give some creature leprosy by injecting it with the organism. Unlike Danielssen, Hansen did not test his idea on himself, as he believed the disease was contagious. He used animals. Leprosy, however, seemed to refuse to cause an infection in anything but a person. (Over the years, scientists have tried to infect parrots, rats, monkeys, rabbits, pigeons, eels, frogs, and guinea pigs, among others, without any success.) So when Hansen, eager to prove to the world that he had found the cause of leprosy, injected a sample containing the tiny rods into rabbits, the rabbits remained as healthy as ever. Frustrated, Hansen decided to try to infect humans, and in the process, he let his zeal run away with him.

The nineteenth-century medical pioneers were quicker to experiment on people than we are today. We know that Danielssen did. Hansen, in 1880, went so far as to try to infect a patient without telling her what he was doing. The patient was a young woman who already had leprosy, so Hansen did not want to give her leprosy but to induce a leprosy infection to grow where he injected the material and thus prove that the material caused the disease. Believing the woman's disease had rendered her eyes insensitive, he decided to inject her eye, feeling certain that if an infection developed, he could cut it out without injuring her sight.

The procedure did cause the young woman pain, however, and she was terrified by what Hansen did. Nearly hysterical, she told the hospital staff about Hansen's experiment. With their encouragement, she sued him for experimenting on her without her consent. It is a testimony to the climate of the times, and how little the will of a young woman who had leprosy was respected, that most of the medical community supported Hansen. He was encouraged to deny the charge that he had not informed her of what he was going to do before the experiment, and if it was his word against that of this woman, surely he would be believed. To Hansen's credit, he did not take that easy route but testified honestly in court that he had not in fact informed the woman of the experiment. The court decided to remove Hansen from his post at the hospital.

Whatever the effect of this ruling, it did not discourage Hansen, nor did it affect his standing in medicine. He continued to work and to be regarded as one of the great leprosy specialists, and eventually he convinced the world that the disease was caused by a microorganism.

THE ARMADILLO TO THE RESCUE

There was still so much more to discover about the disease: although *M. leprae* was the first organism to be found that caused a disease that infected humans, it was not until the late 1940s that the basic guiding principle of its habits was discovered, and this enabled scientists to find an animal other than we humans that could get leprosy.

Why was this important? When trying to identify a drug to treat a disease, scientists usually test possible drugs on animals. While this makes life difficult for the animals they infect, it allows doctors to test risky drugs before giving them to humans and to see what is poisonous, what works, and what does not. *M. leprae,* however, refused to grow in any animal; nor would the bugs grow outside the body in the laboratory.

Since scientists lacked experimental animals, the first leprosy drugs were tested on people: patients at Carville. It was a long and difficult process, and no doubt the patients participated only because they were so desperate for a cure or at least a treatment better than the then-current therapy. The best possible treatment for leprosy patients at the time was the thick, foul-smelling oil from the chaulmoogra plant. Though in many cases it can kill *M. leprae,* if taken orally it was nauseating, and if given in a shot it caused painful sores to form where it was injected: many patients at Carville had to carry a pillow around with them to sit on.

Even though some drugs tested at Carville were known to have drastic side effects, people readily volunteered to try others. In the early 1940s Dr. Guy Faget, a doctor at Carville, heard of a drug called Promin thought to work on leprosy's cousin tuberculosis, and began to test the drug on leprosy patients. At first Promin made the patients so sick that they had to stop taking it orally. So doctors tried again, this time administering the drug intravenously. This was better, but the patients still suffered side effects. Even worse, as the drug would take several months to show any positive results, they saw no change in their condition to make the drug seem worthwhile. People had begun to drop out of the study, giving up hope and going back to the chaulmoogra oil, but some continued to take the drug for six months. Then, finally, the most amazing thing happened. Those who had taken the drug for this amount of time found that their symptoms began to disappear. People whose larynxes had been so affected that they could hardly talk found their voices returning. Ulcers healed; eyesight cleared. What's more, the number of bacilli in their skin samples began to drop precipitously. Promin was killing *Mycobacterium leprae*!

At last there was some hope. At Carville, the discovery of this drug was called a miracle. Without an animal to test it on, the drug had been a risky long shot for patients. But Promin was far from perfect: it could be administered only intravenously— through a needle inserted in a vein—and therefore could be given to patients only in the hospital. It was very unlikely that better drugs could be discovered without an experimental animal. A clue to finding one was uncovered by one young doctor, Paul Brand, a man who was an orthopedic surgeon and found himself drawn further and further into the mysteries of leprosy.

Born to medical missionaries in India, Brand always desired to return to India. He never expected to treat leprosy patients, however. He came back to India to train as a surgeon. It was only after visiting a leprosarium that Brand became fascinated with leprosy. For a surgeon who specialized in hands and feet, leprosy might seem like a nightmare: here were patients who, for the lack of feeling pain, accidentally injured their hands and feet most grue-somely. But that was exactly what motivated Brand: he was desperate to study exactly why the patients became so injured. Paul Brand asked a simple question: Why does leprosy paralyze certain muscles and not others? Brand observed that leprosy patients had very particular disabilities. Certain muscles, and only those muscles, were liable to stop functioning. The muscle that tilts up the foot, and one that bends the hand back at the wrist; one that pulls the thumb over to the palm; the muscle that closes the eyelid—these are some of the muscles leprosy renders useless, not the muscles that lift the head or curl the lip or wrinkle the forehead. Why these muscles and not others? First, Brand asked the doctor who ran the leprosarium this question. He had worked with people with leprosy for years, after all. But the doctor answered that he didn't know; he was a dermatologist, he studied the skin, and no one who studied the muscles and their movement had even asked that question about leprosy before. Brand was astonished: it seemed so obvious a question to explore. So Paul Brand explored it.

Brand spent all his spare time at the leprosarium looking for clues to the mysteries of this disease. It was late one night as he performed an autopsy on a deceased elderly leprosy patient that he found the answer. He didn't even realize at the time the great significance of his discovery. He simply wanted to see what leprosy did to the nerves. Brand carefully exposed the patient's nerves throughout the body, examining the long, white, stringlike bundles of cells that he had become so fascinated with in medical school. Where the nerves were infected with the leprosy bacillus, they were swollen to many times their normal size: the stringlike nerves bulged as thick as a rope. Gazing at these regular swellings, Brand suddenly noticed a pattern. The nerves were infected whenever they passed close to the skin! In the arm, the nerve swelled where it ran just under the skin at the back of the elbow and then narrowed again as it tunneled into the depths of the forearm; in the leg, it swelled where it ran shallowly at the back of the knee; and so on. It would be years before Brand knew a reason for this pattern, which would explain so much about this disease. At the moment of discovery he was so exhausted he had only a tingling intuition that he was onto something big.

Years later, the pattern would come clear: the bacillus did not like it hot! It was only in outside nerves, nerves that were not kept as warm as those snuggled deep in the body, that the bacillus felt comfortable. This also explained why the bacillus invaded the nose and the earlobes and the eyes: they were also comfortably cool. First, using this information, researchers found leprosy grew if injected in the cool feet of mice. Then they found a creature whose whole body is cool enough: it is the cool-bodied armadillo. Leprosy bacilli find armadillos quite a pleasant place in which to live and grow. Today, Carville includes an armadillo research center where scientists can test drugs and vaccines on armadillos. Not good for the armadillos, but very good for humans afflicted with leprosy.

SUFFERING IN THE MIND, NOT IN THE BODY

Brand went on to find surgical ways to repair a leprosy patient's injuries. He was to find ways not only to make paralyzed hands and feet move again but also to restore a normal appearance to patients. As an orthopedic surgeon he had been trained in a tradition that studied deformities and fixed them. In his clinic in India he developed ways to repair club feet. At the leprosy hospital he saw hundreds of crippled hands and feet, hands that were unable to work, feet unable to walk. Although drugs could kill the leprosy bacillus, they could not repair the damage it had already done to the nerves. Patients continued to suffer from injury after

A researcher at Carville with the only animal besides man that is known to contract leprosy

injury to their awkward, painless appendages. The injuries could cause further crippling deformity, which led to greater ostracism. This vicious cycle led one young patient to say to Brand, "I suffer in the mind because I can't suffer in the body."

The more Brand explored the possibilities of fixing these deformities, the more he discovered about why these patients had been neglected. When he asked the hospital where he worked to admit his leprosy patients for hand surgery, he received a variety of responses, but they were all designed to stop him. "Leprosy patients do not pay, and we have a bed shortage." "If word gets out we are treating leprosy patients, no one will want to come to this hospital." Most surprisingly, one doctor said to him, "Don't waste your time; leprosy patients have bad flesh, it is impossible to heal them." "Bad flesh"—these words were to echo in Brand's mind over the next few years as he developed his pioneering surgical methods. This is why no one had explored methods of treatment: doctors, like other people, did not look at leprosy as a disease but as a curse. They dismissed the bodies of lepers as having bad flesh, as being irreparable.

But Brand knew leprosy patients did not have "bad flesh." In the autopsy in which he had discovered the pattern of swollen nerves, he had also seen that the muscles were perfectly healthy. He didn't believe that the disease could make a body bad or good, but that it was simply a matter of overcoming the deficiencies of particular paralyzed nerves. This is how he set out to do it.

Brand saw that only very particular nerves were affected by leprosy, so he concluded if he could get other nerves to guide the movements that were currently paralyzed, he could solve the problem. For instance, some patients were unable to move their thumb into a position opposite their fingers. The thumb could still bend with great strength, but unless it could be bent to meet the fingers over the palm, the hand was unable to grasp. This is a very important movement. You couldn't even turn the pages of this book without grasping. Brand decided to take a muscle that usually bends the ring finger, a muscle he knew was controlled by a nerve that was still working, and attach it to the thumb. First he practiced on cadaver hands, even keeping one in his freezer at home so that he could try different methods again and again. Finally he developed this technique: he made an incision at the base of the ring finger so he could find and cut the stringlike tendon that stretches from the muscle in the forearm to the bone in the finger. Then he made an incision in the wrist and pulled the loose tendon out so that it lay over the palm. Next Brand dug a tunnel under the palm of the hand for the tendon to run on a new path from the muscle to the thumb. After sliding the tendon through its new tunnel, he attached it to the thumb's tendon, with just the right amount of tension to enable the new muscle to work.

After three weeks of recovery, the bandages came off—and the patients could move their thumbs and therefore could again hold a hand, a pen, or a page. There was one small complication. Sometimes it took a while for the brain to work things out: the brain still thought the muscle attached to the thumb was attached to the finger, so at first, when patients tried to move their thumb, they had to think "finger." But in time the brain sorted things out, learning that the muscles had a new configuration.

Brand went on to repair all sorts of deformities in this way. The muscles that lifted the hand and the foot were repaired by ones that turned the hand and foot inward. The muscle that closed the eyelids was repaired by one that closed the jaw. (Until their brains could get used to this new arrangement, the patients' eyes would open and shut in rhythm with their chewing.)

In addition to repairing these functions, Brand found himself performing surgery to restore people's appearance. Often it was the cosmetic repair that patients found most important. One shopkeeper found that even after his disease was arrested and his hands repaired, people refused to come to his shop because he lacked eyebrows! As the lack of eyebrows was a well-known sign of leprosy, Brand decided to make eyebrow grafts, taking bits of hairy scalp and attaching them where the eyebrows should have been. The only catch was that the hair on these eyebrows grew and grew, just like the hair on the head—they would have to be trimmed. But the first pair of new eyebrows Brand fashioned so delighted their new owner, the shopkeeper, that he let them grow down over his eyes, and people flocked to his shop just to see them. Now, with eyebrows, he was considered whole. For the first time, in all the hundreds of years that people have suffered from this disease, not only could their disease be cured but they could be made whole again.

NO MORE LEPROSY?

Today we are in a position Danielssen and Hansen could not have imagined and Stein and Brand could have hoped for only in their wildest dreams. In 1991 the World Health Organization pledged to eliminate leprosy as a public health problem by the end of the century. Although it does not expect to be able to say there is not a single person with leprosy—a very hard claim to make when *M. leprae* can lie hidden in someone's body for as long as fifteen years—WHO does expect to reduce the prevalence of the disease worldwide to less than one case in 10,000 people. With so few cases remaining, the organization hopes leprosy will eventually die out. The reason for this optimism: in the ten years after 1983, when leprosy patients all over the world began to be sought out by health providers and treated with a special combination of drugs, the prevalence of the disease dropped by two thirds. Since the WHO pledge, the number of cases worldwide has fallen from 5.5 million in 1991 to 1.8 million in 1995. In the United States today, there are only 7,000 cases.

We cannot yet assume leprosy is a thing of the past. To be effective, a multidrug regimen must be taken for six months to a year—a very difficult thing for a patient to do. Even more to the point, in order for treatment to be effective, the patient must take the medicine. In order to eradicate leprosy, all the people in the world with the disease must be willing to come forward and be able to receive treatment. They must believe that despite human history, they will not be feared or hated as sinners but will be treated as people with a disease to be cured.

If we do leave leprosy behind someday, we can only hope that we do not forget the lessons of its story: that humans can fear a disease for no good reason; that this fear can lead to great cruelty; and that this fear can lead us to forget to ask the questions that will shed light upon the disease's mysteries. To this day we still do not know precisely how leprosy is transmitted.

PLAGUE

FROM PRAIRIE DOGS TO PEOPLE

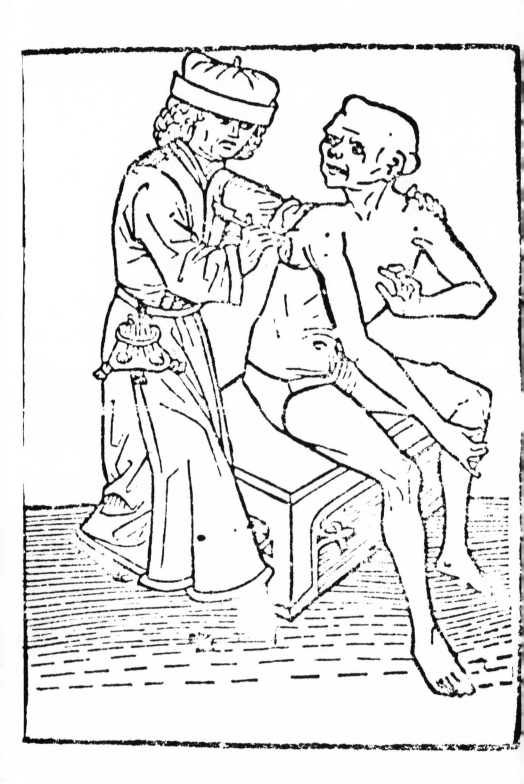

There are far more prairie dogs than humans in northwestern New Mexico, and far more towns of prairie dogs than of people. These prairie dog towns are lively places: prairie dogs run from burrow to burrow on chuckling visits with their neighbors; the watchman calls out a warning cry as a hawk flies overhead, then screams an all-clear when the danger is past; several prairie dogs bark in annoyance at a passing coyote. The New Mexican desert can be noisy with prairie dog social life—except every so often when one prairie dog suddenly sickens and just as suddenly dies, and then another. The disease that kills them so quickly makes its way through the town until every single prairie dog is dead, and the desert is again silent except for the buzzing of flies.

It is 1989, in a hospital in Gallup, New Mexico. An eight-year-old boy has just collapsed on the floor of the men's room. His grandmother brought him to the clinic to be seen for his fever. Now he is curled into a ball and making unintelligible sounds. The emergency room doctor has two guesses. His best guess is plague.

In the fourteenth century, when the Black Death was killing millions of Europeans, physicians gave victims some relief by lancing their buboes

In the twenty years between 1974 and 1993, 164 humans came down with the plague in the state of New Mexico. During that time, plague also appeared in Arizona, Colorado, California, Oregon, Utah, Idaho, Montana, Washington, Wyoming, Nevada, Oklahoma, and Texas: there were three hundred plague cases in all, 237 more than occurred between 1954 and 1973, and in six new states.

It was more than six hundred years ago, in the fourteenth century, that plague swept around the world in a terrifying pandemic known as the Black Death. A pandemic is an epidemic that is very widespread. All our images of plague are colored by the recollections of fear and death left by the European survivors of that global horror. A disease they had never before seen appeared out of nowhere; nearly one half of Europe caught it, and nearly one third died horribly and swiftly. It would be more than five hundred years before the discovery of germs would give people a way to explain such a horror. In their great fear, people responded to the plague in deeds nearly as bizarre and horrible as the disease itself. Today, even though we know the cause and have a treatment for plague, the word still rouses enormous fear.

Plague's secret for a long, successful career in death has been that, unlike smallpox or leprosy, this disease regularly preys upon creatures other than humans. Plague carried by fleas has been known to infect nearly two hundred different animals, including rats, mice, ground squirrels, and cats. And it is in the burrows of wild rodents, such as prairie dogs, that it is believed to live between bouts of infecting humans. These have been very effective hiding places. The only sign of plague's continuing presence might be a dead prairie dog lying in the desert in New Mexico, far from any human eye.

Before plague infected humans, the disease lived among rodents and used their intrepidness to travel across the face of this earth. We have come to know of plague only when the destinies of humans and rodents have crossed.

THE BLACK DEATH

Anyone who dared to venture out upon the streets of Florence in the summer of 1348, even someone who slipped out in the gray light of early dawn to avoid the death carts and the corpse robbers and the plague-inspired bandits, could not avoid the dead. In doorway after doorway they lay in rude piles, father, mother, and children. They had been dragged out and dumped by their neighbors: no one was friend enough to bury the plague dead. By the end of six months, for every resident of Florence still living, at least one would have died. The young as well as the old, the strong as well as the weak all succumbed. In their groins or their armpits rose the painful lumps they called buboes; some grew big as a fist. Black splotches appeared on their skin. From their suffering bodies rose a horrible stench: their sweat and their urine smelled vile. None of the popular treatments, neither bleeding—which was considered beneficial in the mistaken belief that corrupt body substances could be bled out—nor herbal potions, seemed to be of any use. Victims could be dead in a day.

In the fourteenth century, plague moved slowly around the world, beginning sometime around 1330 in the Gobi Desert of Mongolia. This was the second of three plague pandemics in recorded history. The first, beginning in A.D. 541, spread throughout the Mediterranean civilizations. It appeared to those who experienced it to stretch to "the ends of the habitable world." The Black Death was to travel even farther in this second pandemic, making its way east to China, as well as south to India, and west through the Middle East, and on into Europe, in less than twenty years reaching as far as London.

Faster even than the disease traveled the news of it. First, stories of great natural disasters in China made their way to Europe: a drought had scorched the earth, then torrential floods drowned four hundred thousand people. There were deadly earthquakes one after another, and scourges of locusts.

By the end of 1346 people across Europe had heard that these horrible calamities had been followed by the most deadly plague ever known. Death strode across Asia, leaving behind nothing but piles of bodies. Ships were found drifting aimlessly about the sea, their entire crews having perished from the disease.

A year after news of the disease had swept Europe, plague entered cities along the Mediterranean and appeared in Alexandria, Egypt. Along roadsides in Egypt the piles of corpses grew so high bandits used them as cover for ambushes. One traveler in Jerusalem came across a group having a feast in the midst of all this dying. The host explained that he had vowed to hold a feast if the plague should lighten enough for one day to pass without a friend or relative dying. One such day had occurred, so now, for the moment, they feasted.

In 1347 plague entered the port of Messina on the island of Sicily. From there it was a short step to the mainland of Italy. By 1348 it was in Paris, by the end of the year in London. An Italian, Agnolo di Tura, wrote the following about his life in the year 1348:

The mortality in Siena began in May. It was a cruel and horrible thing; and I do not know where to begin to tell of the cruelty and the pitiless ways. It seemed that almost everyone became stupefied by seeing the pain. And it is impossible for the human tongue to recount the awful truth. Indeed, one who did not see such horribleness can be called blessed. And the victims died almost immediately. They would swell beneath the armpits and in their groins, and fall over while talking. Father abandoned child, wife husband, one brother another; for this illness seemed to strike through breath and sight. And so they died. And none could be found to bury the dead for money or friendship. Members of a household brought their dead to a ditch as best they could, without priest, without divine offices. Nor did the death bell sound. And in many places in Siena great pits were dug and piled deep with the multitudes of dead. And they died by the hundreds, both day and night, and all were thrown in those ditches and covered with earth. And as soon as those ditches were filled, more were dug. And I, Agnolo di Tura, called the Fat, buried my five children with my own hands . . . So many died that all believed it was the end of the world.

Sudden death all around them disordered the living. So many were sick and dying that there were too few people to tend the crops, or run the courts, or police the streets. The healthy, too, abandoned their responsibilities, some to flee or to hide, others to live in revelry, drinking and partying away what they thought could be their last days. Some took advantage of the chaos to plunder the homes of the sick or the dead and gather up what wealth they could. They would come upon a house, silent with death, and boldly rob the corpses. There was much to plunder: stores stood empty, riderless horses roamed the streets.

In Florence, Italy, some of those paid to carry away the dead, emboldened by their great risk of death, became fearless brigands. They would burst into the homes of the living and threaten to carry them away along with the dead if they were not appeased with bribes. Between fear of their vicious attacks and fear of the disease, few upright citizens braved the streets of Florence: an expectant quiet settled over the city, broken only by the rattling of the wagons on their rounds to pick up the dead, and the carriages

While the plague raged around them, artists were inspired by its miseries. In this detail from Pieter Brueghel the Elder's painting *The Triumph of Death* (1562), death, depicted as a band of skeletons, comes for young and old, rich and poor

of the wealthy as they hurriedly fled to the country. Behind their closed doors, in their stuffy rooms, everyone wondered: What is killing us, and how can I be saved?

To some, it seemed that the disease passed from one person to another, but they could not explain how it seemed to find its way around even the most elaborate protective measures. And no one could account for how plague could pass from person to person. Some thought it traveled on the breath; others maintained that it took just a look. One physician proposed that "instantaneous death occurs when the aerial spirit escaping from the eyes of the sick man strikes the eyes of a healthy person standing near and looking at the sick, especially when the latter are in agony; for then the poisonous nature of that member passes from one to the other, killing them."

Yet not everyone believed the disease was contagious, that it was spread by some poison or breath or look passing mysteriously from person to person. Some thought that plague, as well as many other diseases, was caused by "bad air," which they referred to as miasma. From the time of the great Greek physician Hippocrates (c. 460–c. 377 B.C.), doctors had argued that people in certain places became ill because the air was poisonous. There had been reports of clouds of pestilential gas floating over China when the plague broke out there. And certainly the winds could be carrying this gas around the planet and with it the awful seeds of plague. Doctors recommended driving off miasma by burning wood scented with aloe or musk, or if you could not afford that, then cypress or laurel. You should sprinkle the floor with vinegar and rose water. If you went out, you could carry a perfume to smell.

No quarantine, no matter how elaborate, could stop a poisonous gas. That would explain why even the citizens of Venice, Italy, who isolated ships at an island in their lagoon for forty days, continued to suffer plague. (Quarantine, which means "forty days" in Italian, was so called because people believed forty days was the period of time necessary for ships to be held to guarantee freedom from infection.) A poisonous miasma could also explain the sudden scarcity of cats, other than the stiff dead ones to be found in the streets. And perhaps miasma had infected the camels that listed and dropped under their loads of trade goods brought from the East and had killed the wolves found lying dead in the forest.

Most believed, whatever its cause, the disease was a curse from God. The signs foretelling its coming had been in the skies: on March 20, 1345, at 1 p.m., Saturn, Jupiter, and Mars were aligned in the house of Aquarius; a ball of fire had been seen in the skies over Paris; in Venice the earth had shaken so violently the bell of St. Mark's rang on its own; there had been falling stars, whales stranded on the beach, hot winds blowing out of the south. And the imagined reasons for God's punishment seemed many to those who looked around: everywhere one could find greed, lechery, gluttony, and drunkenness. To those convinced that their death was a just curse, what could they do to prevent God's justice? But not to do anything, to simply wait for death, was too horrible. People wore amulets of every kind: those who could afford them wore sapphires for protection, those who couldn't wore amber; others wore amulets of arsenic. Some carried magic words written like this as a charm:

```
A  B  R  A  C  A  D  A  B  R  A
  A  B  R  A  C  A  D  A  B  R
   A  B  R  A  C  A  D  A  B
    A  B  R  A  C  A  D  A
     A  B  R  A  C  A  D
      A  B  R  A  C  A
       A  B  R  A  C
        A  B  R  A
         A  B  R
          A  B
           A
```

In Germany, a movement began that sought to appease God's wrath through group mortification; it was known as the Brotherhood of the Flagellants. The flagellants would march, sometimes as many as one thousand strong, from town to town, each dressed in a black robe with a red cross, and carrying a metal-tipped leather scourge. They marched in silence two abreast, the men first, followed by the women. When they entered a town, they went first to the church and prayed their special litany. Then they marched to the town square to perform their bloody rite. Surrounded by the people of the town, they formed a large circle, stripped to the waist, pulled out their whips, and began to beat themselves. They beat themselves in rhythm while chanting their

A French doctor's anti-plague outfit from 1720: a leather robe, a mask with crystal eyepieces and a beak filled with perfumes to ward off plague poisons and death stench, and a cane to point at the bodies of the sick

orſtellung des Doct. Chicogneau Lantzlers der Vniverſitael zu Montpe.
r welcher A: 1720. vom Könige in Franckreich nach Marſeille geſchicket worden

flagellants' hymn. Each tried to outdo the others in the vicious-ness of the beating, until they were senseless, and hardly felt the pain.

The flagellants performed this rite twice a day and once at night. To join the group, one had to swear to scourge oneself three times a day for thirty-three days, a day for each year in the life of Jesus Christ. They marched from town to town, making their lodging in monasteries, and, at first, hurting no one but them-selves and providing a diversion for the frightened peasants. As time went on, however, the flagellants began to direct their vio-lence at others: they began to lead a persecution of Jews.

In searching for a reason for the plague, some looked to the strangers in their midst and accused them of causing the disease. In Spain, for instance, Arab people were so accused; in Portugal, religious pilgrims. But all across northern Europe, it was Jewish people who were accused of bringing on the plague. Jews already suffered from discrimination and persecution in many places: they were barred from owning land, from being craftsmen or practicing many other occupations. In southern France, where the plague accusations seem to have begun, Jews were already being killed in mass attacks in the years before the plague. The plague gave this hatred an excuse, and the hatred gave people's fear of the plague a focus.

In Chillon, France, in September of 1348, a Jewish man was put upon the rack and asked to admit that Jews had poisoned the wells and so caused the disease. When the man, in his agony, agreed with his torturer in order to end his pain, his false confes-sion was written down as truth and sent to all the neighboring towns as proof of Jewish guilt. Mass bloodshed followed. In Basel, Switzerland, all the Jews were boarded up into wooden buildings and burned alive. In Strasbourg, Germany, as two thousand Jews were marched to their execution, people stole the clothes off their

A fifteenth-century woodcut showing Jews being burned to death by those who accused them of causing plague

backs. German Jews were murdered in Stuttgart, in Freiburg, in Dresden and Baden. Jews in Frankfurt fought back, killing two hundred of their persecutors. In response, as many as twelve thousand Jews were murdered there.

The flagellants joined in the persecution: in each town they visited they instigated the murder of Jews. It was not until the worst of the outbreak was over, three years later, that the persecution was to stop. That Jews and Christians alike died of the plague did not give pause to the persecutors, nor did the fact that no one seemed to catch the disease from well water. Hatred, not reason, inspired their actions. After three years and 350 massacres, tens of thousands of Jews had been killed and more than two hundred Jewish communities had been annihilated.

Strangely enough, no one seems to have noticed the rats. Hardly one of the plague chroniclers mentions these rodents, which must have been lying dead in the dark back streets, and in the walls of poor homes, and occasionally swept by a disgusted mother out of a kitchen. No one seems to have noticed that many rats were dying—rats that could have nimbly found their way ashore, even from a quarantine boat.

THE SHRINKING WORLD

About one hundred and fifty years before the Black Death, the empire of Genghis Khan and his Mongol warriors began to stretch across Asia, eventually to encompass much of China and Russia. The empire bound together these vast lands with a network of messengers and traders broader and swifter than any that had been seen before. Caravans traveled new northern routes across the great dry plains of Central Asia known as the steppes, and messengers on swift ponies traveled one hundred miles a day. They made the world smaller and brought into contact people and creatures that had never before met.

It seems very possible that, borne in the saddlebags of these swift Mongol ponies, and in the sacks of grain carried to feed the traders on their way, and in booty stolen by ransacking Mongol warriors, traveled the plague.

The plague has a nimble home: when the bacillus that causes the disease is not infecting a dying human, or some other larger creature, it lives in the body of a flea. A plague epidemic depends upon the presence of rats and fleas because bubonic plague—the most common form of the disease, named for the buboes it causes—cannot spread from person to person without a flea to carry it. Occasionally, the type of flea that likes to bite humans can be the culprit, but most of the time it is the rat flea, and the plague must go from rat to flea to human.

The rat flea prefers the body of a creature like a rat to bite for its dinner of blood, but if another body—such as a human one—is within leaping distance, it will do. The flea leaps and bites, and in its bite it disperses the plague. In fact, the flea is eager to bite because the plague has made it very hungry. Plague germs multiplying inside the flea block its stomach, leaving the flea insatiable. It bites and bites, drinking feverishly, as it tries to satisfy itself. For plague, this is ideal, since the blocked flea vomits the blood it desperately drinks right back into the wound it has made in its host's flesh, and along with the blood, plague germs. The flea bite becomes an injection of plague bacilli.

It appears that plague lived in the burrows of wild rodents near the mountainous intersection of China, India, and Burma. Plague traveled from rodent to rodent, carried by the flea. If all the rodents in an area died of the disease, leaving all the fleas to starve to death, plague could still survive in the dirt of the rodent burrows for as long as five years. If during that time another rodent and its flea companions happened to move in, plague was ready to spread again. Plague probably lived in these mountains for thousands of years, but it could travel only as far as a rat or flea could take it. Although nimble, plague's short-legged hosts were not long-distance travelers, and the occasional person that they infected did not go far from home in his or her life. Then came the Mongols, who invaded those Himalayan foothills in 1252. And a Mongol caravan may have camped next to a field rat burrow. And a field rat might have crept into a sleeping trader's sack of grain. Or a flea may have leaped from a field rat's back onto a rat riding in a messenger's saddlebag. We don't know exactly how it happened, but we do know that plague now makes its home in the burrows of rodents all across the steppes of Asia, and that while the Mongols ruled, plague began to see the world.

It was not just the Mongol caravans that were making the world a smaller place. Sailing ships trading in the Mediterranean were voyaging all the way to Northern Europe. Better-designed ships could now sail throughout the winter. By the end of the thirteenth century they could sail from the Black Sea port of Kaffa throughout the Mediterranean, through the Straits of Gibraltar, and on up to the North Sea ports. When the ships pulled into port, among those to disembark were the black rats running down the ropes that fastened the boats to the wharves. Native to India, they were the favored host of the flea that carried the plague.

The rats that ran off the sailing ships arrived in a Europe that had swollen to the bursting point. Europe's population had grown by leaps and bounds in the previous few centuries, so that there were now more people than there was food to feed them or wood to house them. And in the years approaching the 1340s, bad winters had decimated food crops, leaving even less food for an already hungry continent.

When the first plague-infested ship landed at Messina on the island of Sicily, there were as yet uninfected rats onshore to host the fleas, and starving humans to succumb to the plague. The Black Death had arrived.

Plague bacilli are terrible little toxin factories. The heat of the human body signals the thousands of bacilli injected by the flea to go into special production: they begin to make poisons specifically designed to help them bore their way into human cells. If the human's immune-system cells manage to kill some of them, the germs release more poisons from their dying bodies. Meanwhile, they work their way into the body's fluid drainage system, called the lymphatic system, to travel. If the flea bite was on the leg, the lymph drainpipes carry plague to the lymph nodes in the groin. If the bite is on the hand, plague rides the pipes to the armpit nodes. In the nodes, the filtering centers of the lymphatic system, a massive battle begins to take place. The bacilli excrete toxins, the body sends immune-system cells, and the node swells with the dead of both armies and coagulated blood. It forms a bubo, a hard lump that can reach the size of an orange, a lump that can last for several days and is so painful it can almost drive one mad. If the person is lucky, the bubo will burst, leaving a horrible open wound, somewhat relieving the pain and perhaps marking the beginning of recovery.

Even without treatment, as many as one quarter to one half of bubonic plague victims will survive. But in an unlucky one out of twenty victims the bacilli will find their way to the lungs and become pneumonic plague. The lungs are an excellent place for plague to grow, and it will rapidly infect the entire lung surface. One day the victim has a headache and fever and the next is coughing up bloody sputum. The lungs are so rapidly destroyed the body cannot get enough oxygen and the hands and feet begin to turn black. Without treatment, the patients will certainly die that very day or the next. And every cough from the victim's infected lungs will disperse plague bacilli into the air. Unlike bubonic plague, this form of infection needs no flea. All those who inhale those bacilli are vulnerable to developing plague in their own lungs.

To the witnesses of the plague, living in their small towns, none of this was evident. They didn't even notice the dead rats, much less the tiny fleas. They only saw the horrible inexplicable deaths of those people around them. While plague would return again and again to ravage people in Europe, Asia, and Africa, it would be hundreds of years before they were to consider that such devastation was wrought by the tiny invisible living creatures we know as germs.

GERM HUNTING IN THE WILDS OF AN EPIDEMIC

Five and a half centuries after the onset of the Black Death, in 1894, a plague epidemic that had been making its way across

Multituds flying from London by water in boats & barges.

Flying by land.

Burying the dead with a bell before them.   Searchers

Carts full of dead to bury.

When it struck London in 1665, the Black Death pandemic killed nearly one out of every six citizens

China for nearly fifty years reached the busy international port of Hong Kong. This caught the attention of Western Europe and came to be called the beginning of the Third Pandemic. Since 1665, when the Black Death pandemic had its last hurrah in the Great Plague of London, Western Europe had been generally plague-free. In other parts of the world, such as Eastern Europe, the Middle East, India, and Africa, periodic deadly outbreaks of the disease continued to occur, but Western Europeans had felt safe from plague. Plague in Hong Kong, however, threatened that security.

This new threat again took advantage of an innovation in travel: the steamship, which came more and more into use on ocean routes in the nineteenth century, gave plague a new way to see the world. Steam could power much bigger ships than sail could—the better to carry more rats aboard—and ships that didn't depend upon the wind could reach more places faster. Now a plague infection on board a ship could travel from rat to rat to rat and not kill them all before reaching the other side of the ocean: some rats remained alive to sneak ashore, bearing their gift of plague. Plague could take a steamship from Hong Kong to just about anywhere in the world. It seemed the events of five hundred years before could be repeating themselves. But while, five hundred years before, thinkers had looked to the heavens for a reason for plague, and recorded the falling stars, the alignment of the planets, or the ball of fire in the sky, this time they looked through microscopes into the world of germs.

By the end of the nineteenth century, scientists had already identified the germs that cause diphtheria, tetanus, botulism, cholera, tuberculosis, leprosy, and malaria, among others. The new science of bacteriology—the study of bacteria—was off and running. To bacteriologists, the world was full of diseases caused by germs. All they had to do was identify a disease, find the germ, name it after themselves, and go down in history. Armed with their microscopes, two bacteriologists set out after plague. But when they arrived in Hong Kong in 1894, the two had very different receptions. One, Shibasaburo Kitasato, was a highly regarded academic professor with an international reputation who had been trained by the great German scientist Robert Koch, a founding father of the study of microbes. The Japanese doctor was confident that he could achieve fame in Hong Kong. He arrived with a team of five, was offered space in the British-run hospital to set up his laboratory, and was guaranteed access to the corpses of plague victims for autopsy.

The other was a Swiss, who came not from Europe but from nearby Indochina (in southeast Asia), where he had been living for four years. Alexandre Yersin's career had started out in the lab of the French scientist Louis Pasteur, another founding father of microbiology. Yersin's early work promised a great career in academic science, on a par with Kitasato's, but at the age of twenty-four he had given that all up to travel to Indochina and live the life of an explorer. Yersin made three great journeys of exploration into the uncharted wilds of this French colony, one by foot, one by canoe, and one by elephant. He drew up maps for these wild lands, and treated the diseases suffered by the mountain villagers he came across—malaria and cholera as well as plague. Now he had been sent by the French government to Hong Kong to try to discover the cause of this scourge.

When Yersin arrived, it seemed that he had stepped into the shadow of Kitasato: Yersin had only a bamboo hut in which to work, all the corpses for autopsy went to Kitasato, and for assistance Yersin had but one servant. Nevertheless, with an explorer's ingenious tenacity, he bribed some sailors who had been employed as

gravediggers, and convinced them to let him remove the buboes
from the corpses before they were buried. He wrote in his journal:

> With the help of Father Vigano, I try to persuade some English
> sailors, whose duty it is to bury the dead from the city and other hos-
> pitals, to let me take the buboes from the dead before they are
> buried. A few dollars conveniently distributed and the promise of
> a good tip for every case have a striking effect. The bodies before they
> are carried to the cemetery are deposed for one or two hours
> in a cellar. They are already in their coffins in a bed of lime.
>
> The coffin is opened. I move the lime to clear the crural [thigh]
> region. The bubo is exposed; within less than a minute I cut it away
> and run to my laboratory.

When, in his hut, he peered through his microscope at the bits
of tissue, Yersin found masses of an oval-shaped germ. Lo and
behold, when he slipped this bug inside his mice and guinea pigs,
they died of plague. Yersin named the bug *Pasteurellis pestis* after
his teacher Pasteur.

Meanwhile, Kitasato, in his autopsies, also found a germ
swarming in the tissue he examined, which he believed to be the
cause of the disease. He wrote a paper describing his find, and as
he was so well respected it was published in the widely read
English medical journal *The Lancet*. Yersin's report of his work,
on the other hand, was available only to those who read a French-
language journal with a much smaller circulation. But later experiments by both Yersin and Kitasato soon revealed that the germ
that Kitasato was describing was not the one that caused plague.
It appeared that the portions of tissue that Kitasato had examined
had been invaded by another microbe, one that commonly lives
just about everywhere and is a relative of the bug that causes strep

throat. This microbe liked to grow at a higher temperature than the plague bacillus. In his well-equipped lab, Kitasato was able to keep his samples in an incubator, which kept them warmed to just this temperature. Yersin, meanwhile, had no such opportunity; his samples sat around in the same tropical heat that everyone endured—but that was ten degrees Celsius cooler than the temperature in the incubator. At this temperature, the plague germs thrived. So it was the plague germ that Yersin continued to observe and describe in his investigations, while Kitasato's work was led off track by a microbial impostor. Eventually, the name of the plague germ was changed to *Yersinia pestis* to honor the man who discovered it.

At the time, far more important than who had found the disease was how to use this information to stop the simmering epidemic. The world set out to stop the plague that had hopped on the steamers roaring into Hong Kong's busy port and steaming out to travel the world. But no one knew that plague had stowed away inside furry passengers: Yersin had found the germ, but he did not know about its collaboration with the rat and the flea. And knowing that a germ caused the disease would not prevent fear and prejudice from standing in the way of fighting the epidemic.

SAN FRANCISCO SAYS IT ISN'T SO

Plague arrived in San Francisco in March of the year 1900, its first visit to the continental United States. The disease first showed itself by killing a Chinese man in Chinatown. When an autopsy, and the death of lab rats, guinea pigs, and a monkey who had been infected with his germs, left no question that the disease was plague, the medical authorities attempted to take action. They ran right into fear, prejudice, and greed.

San Francisco was a booming seaport town in 1900: sea trade was its business. A plague epidemic would be the undoing of all that, for the city would be quarantined, and huge sums of money would be lost. So business leaders simply refused to acknowledge the epidemic or else claimed that it was merely a disease of the Chinese. And the medical authorities, not yet realizing the role of rats, as well as suffering from prejudice, took action against the Chinese rather than against the plague.

First, police surrounded Chinatown so that no one could leave. Then railroads, streetcars, and ferries were ordered to refuse to allow anyone who looked Chinese to ride on them. A judge's order was necessary to prevent the Board of Health from moving all the Chinese to an island and burning Chinatown down. All these measures ignored the fact that plague infects humans of all colors, shapes, and sizes and that the real villain, the rat, ran freely back and forth between the policemen's legs and out into the city.

Meanwhile, all but one of the city's newspapers refused to print news of plague. The governor of California, in the interest of business, declared there was no plague in San Francisco, fired the Board of Health members who kept insisting that there was, accused the doctor who was reporting plague of having infected the experimental animals with plague himself, and proclaimed that it should be made a felony to report that plague was present in the city.

The federal government finally intervened, and in January of 1901, almost a year after the disease had first broken out, sent an expert commission to San Francisco. Much to the governor's consternation, its members set up in a lab in the University of California's medical school. The governor promptly made arrangements to throw them out of the state institution, so they moved into a small room provided by the Board of Health.

Their report, issued March 6, 1901, concluded that plague was in fact roaming the city. The reaction was to attack Chinatown with every kind of germ-killing cleaner known. Twelve hundred houses were treated. Household goods were moved out to sit in the sunshine. Walls were scrubbed with mercuric chloride and rooms fumigated for forty-eight hours with sulfur dioxide gas. All of this probably sent the rats running for the hills, carrying plague with them.

In the end, plague killed 122 people in the four years it contin-ued to roam the city. A smaller proportion of the people in the city were infected than during the Black Death, perhaps because more-modern houses were less vulnerable to rats and fleas, but of those infected, just as many died. There was still no treatment for plague.

With the use of little rat legs to get around, the disease was not confined to Chinatown, or even to the city borders, but went on out into the countryside, and there, when the city rats met the wild rodents of the California countryside, they presented them with plague. Just as plague carried to Mongolia by the Mongols traveled from rodent burrow to rodent burrow out into the great steppes of Asia, plague from San Francisco traveled out to the ground squir-rels of the suburbs, and then to the prairie dogs of the desert of the American West. Some people helped the wandering rodents move from state to state: ranchers who found prairie dogs a nuisance would drive hundreds of miles to find sick prairie dogs to bring home and give the plague to the ones on their ranch. Plague spread as far north as Canada, as far south as Mexico, and as far east as Oklahoma. This creeping infection went on to find its way into 300 people in the twenty years between 1974 and 1993, including one eight-year-old boy in Gallup, New Mexico.

ON LITTLE RAT FEET

It was in India that plague hit the hardest during the Third Pan-demic, arriving in Bombay in 1896 and killing ten million people in the next twelve years, and it was here that researchers finally came to realize the rat connection. Eight hundred years before, in a Hindu holy book called the Bhagavata Purana, Indian scholars wrote that plague was a disease of rats. In China, for hundreds of years, people had believed that the death of rats foretold the death of men. But somehow this wisdom was ignored or forgotten and ultimately had to be relearned.

In fact, when a man named Paul Louis Simmond, working much like Yersin, without sophisticated equipment, sitting in a hut in a tropical country far from home, made the brilliant connection of the disease with the rat and the flea, his conclusions were ridiculed at first. Yet this finding would be the key to controlling the disease. Years later, drugs would be found to fight the infection, but it was Simmond's finding that allowed us to control plague epidemics. Although he published his work in 1898, it was not until years later, when his work was replicated by other scientists, that the connection was recognized throughout the world.

Finally we understood that the trail of human deaths left by plague was only half of the story. Somewhere in dark burrows were deaths we did not see. Rodents were getting sick and dying. When humans came within a flea hop of a rat, when a rat rode home with a Mongol, or when a ship carried rats to overcrowded ports, then humans came down with the plague.

After all these years, when plague struck San Francisco for the second time, in 1907, the city responded by going after the rats. The city spent half a million dollars on rat extermination, and offered a reward of five cents for every rat brought, "dead or alive," to the Health Department. Thirty-five thousand cards, called kitchen cards, describing how to keep a clean house and to catch rats safely, were printed and given out to schoolchildren to take home and hang up in their kitchen.

Plague fighters studied the ways of the rat to learn how to make ratproof ships. Rats cannot jump more than three feet, they wrote, and cannot climb up around a smooth nine-inch overhang. Then they used this information to build ratproof ships and storage places. They cut off the migration of rats around the world: since the pandemic that began in Hong Kong in 1894, plague has never again traveled around the world.

GALLUP, NEW MEXICO

Although plague no longer travels the world, it is far from gone. Plague lives today among rodents in Asia, Africa, and the Americas. But today we know where it hides and how to attack it. In New Mexico, when the emergency room doctor saw the feverish eight-year-old boy who had just passed out on the men's room floor, even though his fingers could not find a bubo under the boy's arm or inside his leg he guessed from the boy's other symptoms that prairie dogs might be dying in the New Mexican desert and that this boy might have plague. He placed the boy in strict isolation and started him on plague antibiotics immediately.

It had been more than forty years after Yersin found the plague

To celebrate the end of a plague control campaign in 1908, San Franciscans demonstrate that their city is so clean a meal can be eaten in the streets

bacillus and Simmond published his paper implicating rats that science first came upon a treatment for plague that worked. In the early years of the twentieth century, some researchers began to explore whether chemicals could be found that would kill germs and not people. One of the very first such anti-microbial agents discovered was tried against plague in 1938. It saved nine out of ten sufferers from bubonic plague, but, unfortunately, could do nothing for those with the pneumonic form. Then, in 1944, an even better plague killer called streptomycin, an antibiotic, was discovered. Antibiotics are chemical substances produced by microbes to kill other microorganisms; scientists harnessed these chemicals as germ-killing drugs. If given within fifteen hours of the first symptoms, streptomycin could save even those with pneumonic plague. In Gallup, New Mexico, the doctor quickly gave the boy another antibiotic since discovered to be effective against the disease—chloramphenicol. Seven hours later, the boy was able to speak. Five days later, his fever was gone and he was well.

In 1994 earthquakes rocked western India, followed by devastating floods, and on the heels of these two disasters came an outbreak of plague. This sequence of events was eerily reminiscent of the events centuries before, when, following great earthquakes and floods, the Black Death first took hold in China. Just as happened at the time of the Black Death, news of the plague spread fear around the world. But this time we did not look upon the disease as a sign of God's wrath, foretold by the natural disasters; this time we saw the rats. The earthquakes, we realized, had destroyed farmers' grain storage buildings, and with easy access to grain the rats grew fat and happy and reproduced quickly. Then the floods washed garbage and dead animals out into the streets, creating more food for the rats. When the plague came, we knew what to do: ratcatchers poured into the streets and antibiotics poured into India. Swift action ended the outbreak.

When plague broke out in India in 1994, health officials in Bombay offered seventeen cents for each dead rat brought in by citizens. Here a city worker holds one of the more than four hundred rats he collected in one day

Plague is a disease we have not been able to eradicate, and one we may never be rid of: in 1995, the first case of plague that was resistant to all known plague drugs infected a sixteen-year-old boy in Madagascar. Even without effective treatment, the boy managed to fight the disease off, and recovered, but health officials remain concerned. Out there among the fleas and rodents how many more resistant germs might there be? No one knows, but at least we know where to look, and with rat-catchers, and flea poison, and as many new drugs as we can find, when plague comes again, we will be ready to fight.

TUBERCULOSIS

THE RETURN OF THE SLOW KILLER

upfen und Diphterie werden di
tragen.) Darum **Taschentuch** vor
d beim Husten.

illst du wissen, wie du dich
rkulose schützen kannst, so merk
ndes: zunächst achte darauf, daß

Youth grows pale, and spectre-thin, and dies . . ." The poet who wrote these words, John Keats, was only twenty-four when he first coughed up blood. When Keats came home feverish one night, the friend he was staying with urged him to go to bed at once. No sooner did he lie down than he gave a hacking cough that brought with it the unmistakable taste of blood. The candle he lit confirmed his expectations: it revealed a bright red spot on his pillow. "That drop of blood is my death-warrant," Keats said calmly to his friend; "I must die." Frightened, his friend ran out into the cold February night for a doctor in the first of many attempts to save young Keats over the next year. But all attempts were useless. Tuberculosis germs could have been hiding in Keats's lungs since childhood; by the time the disease revealed itself, leaving its red signature on his pillow, the battle was already lost.

Keats knew this all too well: as a boy of fourteen, he had cared for his mother when she lay dying of tuberculosis. He allowed no one else to cook her meals, and sat with her through the night in a

"Cover your mouth when you cough!" admonished a tuberculosis control brochure distributed in Germany, in the early twentieth century

room with the doors and windows shut tight against drafts. When he was twenty-three, he did the same for his youngest brother. In those long hours, Keats both breathed in countless numbers of *Mycobacterium tuberculosis,* the germ that causes the disease, and learned firsthand the details of how he himself would die.

It has been estimated that in Keats's day, the beginning of the nineteenth century, one quarter of all Europeans died young of tuberculosis. At that time, the creative were considered especially vulnerable: one could hardly claim to be an artist without a bloody handkerchief. The poet Lord Byron, who did not have the disease, once went so far as to wish he would die of tuberculosis because, he said, the ladies would all say, "Look at that poor Byron, how interesting he looks in dying!"

Of course, once Byron was dead, the ladies would not matter, but part of the allure of tuberculosis was that dying went on for years: the thin, flushed, and feverish look was considered romantic, and one was not always too sick to enjoy being so perceived. But this slow, creeping death is also what has made tuberculosis so terrible. Like its relative leprosy, tuberculosis reproduced much more slowly than most germs. This made it difficult to diagnose, concealed the fact that it was contagious, and made it hard to study in the laboratory. Tuberculosis is stealthy: after it enters a body, the germ will wait as long as it takes, ten days or fifty years, for the moment the host is weak enough to attack. When tuberculosis does attack, the infected person feels tired, gradually more and more so, but does not know why. Tuberculosis gives no outward sign of its presence until too late. Before we learned how to probe the body for evidence of the disease with X rays and skin tests, the bright red spot of coughed-up blood was the first definitive sign, and by then tuberculosis was well established.

Today, five decades after a cure for the disease was found, tuberculosis, known as TB for short, kills more people than any other single germ. It is the largest single cause of death from infectious disease in the United States. Worldwide, three million people die from it each year; over eight million become infected. In little more than the time it takes you to read this sentence, another person will die of TB.

HIDING PLACES

The doctor who rushed to Keats's bedside that snowy evening could do very little. Both doctor and patient understood that the bright red color of the blood on the pillow meant it was oxygen-rich blood from an artery, freshly bleeding into the lung. But neither could tell for sure how badly damaged the lungs were, or what caused them to bleed so. The doctor could order no X rays, and he did not even have a stethoscope in his bag to explore the lungs sucking air into Keats's thin chest. The stethoscope had just been invented and was still considered an eccentric instrument. To examine the lungs, the doctor could either place his cold ear against Keats's hot, feverish chest and listen, or he could tap on Keats's skin, moving down each side of his chest in a line of taps, until he heard the hollow drumlike sound of healthy lungs give way to a dull thud where the lungs were too congested to breathe.

From this examination he concluded that the poet's lungs were fine. The germ fooled the doctor, even if it did not fool Keats. The doctor pulled out his surgical lancet, pierced Keats's arm, and applied the current therapy for such a fever: he allowed Keats to bleed. In fact, this treatment could only have further weakened Keats's body and helped tuberculosis along. The doctor could not find and attack the tiny enemy Keats breathed in years before.

The rod-shaped bacilli that cause tuberculosis, each just two millionths of a meter long, can travel comfortably in the tiny moist particles that ride in one's breath. These droplets, carrying one to three bacilli each, are small enough to float in the air and can stay suspended for hours, ready to be sucked into another person's lung. A larger particle would get caught in the mucus that lines the airways to trap such invaders. But these tiny droplets slip through into the tiny mucus-free air sacs that make up the sponge-like lung. Although the bacilli have evaded the mucus, the body does have another trap waiting. In the air sacs, cells known as macrophages (from the Greek words for "big eater") lie in wait to eat such foreign invaders. Unfortunately, unlike most bugs, TB bacilli are very comfortable in the belly of the macrophages. The chemicals inside the macrophage that kill most germs do not harm *Mycobacterium tuberculosis.* If they were properly armed by the immune system, the macrophages could kill TB, but it takes the immune system three weeks to notice a tuberculosis infection. Meanwhile tuberculosis reproduces happily inside the "big eaters."

When finally armed, macrophages can kill the bacilli, but they often die themselves in the process, release their chemicals in the lung, and kill lung cells. A cheesy mass of dead cells forms in the midst of the healthy pink spongy lung. And sometimes a few bacilli survive even the armed macrophages. These lie waiting for a moment of weakness when they can begin to reproduce again. When their host is severely overworked or underfed or very sick or takes up smoking, they start to proliferate. The host's body resents the sudden growing presence of hundreds of tiny bacilli and orders the immune system to destroy them, but, in the process, it destroys nearby lung cells as well. Eventually blood vessels in the tattered lungs wear through and the host coughs bright red blood. Death can follow. Sometimes such a large vessel is damaged that the patient bleeds to death, or the soup of bacilli and dead lung cells can spill into the bloodstream, causing a deadly toxic reaction. Or sometimes the lung is so eroded it collapses upon itself like a popped balloon.

While tuberculosis most often infects the lungs, the germ has many hiding places in the body. The lungs are a favored spot because of the ease with which the germ can travel on the air into the lungs, and the steady supply of oxygen that it receives there, but tuberculosis has also been known to travel into the body in contaminated, unpasteurized milk and set up shop in the intestines. Sometimes tuberculosis hides in the lymph nodes of the neck and swells the throat like a horrible case of mumps; at other times it hides in the voice box and steals the voice. It can infect the kidneys, the skin, the blood, or the lining of the brain.

Tuberculosis can also infect the bones, and it is in the bones that we can read its history. The lungs and throats of the dead decay with time and leave no discernible trace, but bones riddled with characteristic cavities where they have been eroded by TB have remained for thousands of years as proof of infection. In 1907, in Heidelberg, Germany, archaeologists found the six-thousand-year-old spine of a young man whose fourth and fifth thoracic vertebrae, which are high up in the back, were eaten away. His spine had collapsed forward under the weight of his head, giving him the sharp-angled hump that is the telltale sign of tuberculosis of the spine. In addition to the bones, over the centuries artists have left us images of these high, pointy hunchbacks. Images or bones found in Egypt, China, Peru, California, and Tennessee tell us that tuberculosis, unlike smallpox, had traveled around the world and to the Americas long before Columbus. If there had been any doubt, in 1994 scientists found tuberculosis DNA, the chemical fingerprint of the germ, in a nine-hundred-year-old Peruvian mummy.

LOOKING INTO THE BODY

From the beginning, the problem for physicians treating TB was to find out that the germ was there, before the bones collapsed or

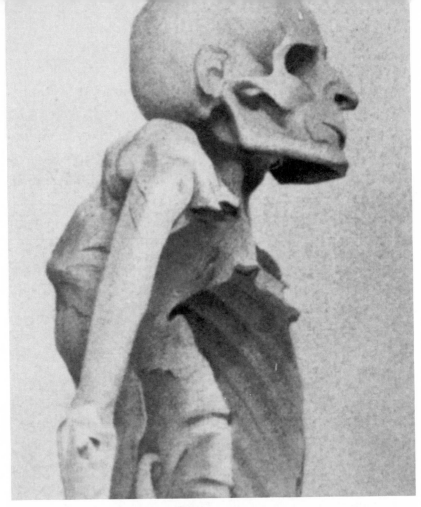

The hump high in the back of this three-thousand-year-old Egyptian mummy indicates a spine crumpled by tuberculosis

the lungs became cheesy and tattered. The diseased tissues were impenetrable; those caring for sufferers could not see in but could see only what came out. The ancient Greeks developed tests to analyze what the tubercular patient coughed up. In one test, the physician would have the patient spit into a copper vessel filled with seawater; if the sputum sank, death was near. In another, he dripped the sputum on hot coals; if it smelled of rotten meat, again, death was near. But the condition of the lungs themselves was hidden deep inside the chest of the living.

As Keats lay feverish in his bed, there were thousands of other young European men and women who were also in peril, tuberculosis replicating relentlessly deep in their bodies, as yet undisclosed. Among them was a young French doctor, René Laënnec. In his short, illness-ridden life, he would bring to the world a window into the chest by inventing the stethoscope.

Like Keats, Laënnec lost his mother when he was young, just five years old, to what historians believe was tuberculosis; and also like Keats, Laënnec was to see his brother die of the same disease. After their mother's death, the Laënnec boys had been raised by their uncle, who was a doctor. It was because of his guardian's influence that when he was still a small, frail, freckled boy, Laënnec determined to make medicine his career.

This was a time when medicine was becoming more scientific; that is, doctors were exploring by careful observation and experiment the ways that the body worked and how to treat disease. Doctors in Europe were beginning to look upon disease differently. The physicians of ancient Greece considered disease as part of the natural world rather than the spiritual. They based their study upon direct observation: what was part of the physical world one could learn about by observing with one's own eyes. But in the Middle Ages in Europe, the followers of the Greek tradition began to put more faith in what was written in the old books than in what they could see. For instance, although, unlike most Greek anatomists, medieval physicians dissected dead bodies, and therefore had the opportunity to correct some big mistakes in the Greek books on anatomy, instead they had the Greek books on anatomy read out loud when they dissected, and tried to describe what they saw the same way the Greeks believed it to be. They could have seen with their own two eyes that the Greeks were wrong about things—that there were no holes in the heart where the Greeks said there were, for example—but they insisted upon believing the books instead of their own eyes.

It was from the 1600s onward in Europe that scientists gradually began to pay more attention to their own observations. They perceived disease not as a curse, nor as due to the movements of the planets, but as a part of the natural, earthly world. And they did not look to the writings of the ancient Greeks to explain this phenomenon: they believed that they could discover the truth about disease through their own experience. For instance, Laën-

Self-portrait of a tubercular René Laënnec in 1820, six years before his death

nec, reflecting on the common observation that tuberculosis patients often felt better when they were at the seashore, wondered if the seaweed on the beach was the key to curing the disease. He decided to see for himself by conducting an experiment. He laid seaweed on the floor around the hospital beds of several patients and gave them seaweed tea for four months and watched to see if they improved. The ward did begin to smell like the seashore, and the patients said they felt better, but Laënnec saw no conclusive improvement. Laënnec considered the treatment a failure, but felt he had learned something: he had learned that seaweed was not what made the seashore healthful. Thus the experiment was a success.

It was the desire to make better observations that inspired Laënnec to devise the stethoscope. Before Keats's century, the only way doctors investigated to see if lungs were full of fluid and therefore diseased was by the Greek physician Hippocrates' method of shaking the patient by the shoulders and listening for a splash. In 1761 the doctor son of an Austrian innkeeper, Leopold Auenbrugger, came up with an ingenious new idea. Just as his father had rapped on the side of casks of wine or beer to tell how much was in them, so could a person rap on the side of someone's chest to tell how fluid-filled the lungs were. The healthy, empty lung made a sound like a drum when the chest was tapped, but the damaged lung made a dull thud. Auenbrugger's idea was dismissed at first, but was revived around 1800, at the time when Laënnec was studying medicine.

Both Auenbrugger's method, known as percussion, and the other available way to investigate the chest, listening by pressing the ear against the skin, had their drawbacks. Women's breasts could make both methods impractical and indelicate, and fat on a patient of either sex could get in the way. But it was just these obstacles that led Laënnec to discover a better way of investigating the chest altogether. This is how he wrote about his moment of discovery:

> *In 1816, I was consulted by a young woman laboring under general symptoms of diseased heart, and in whose case percussion and the application of the hand were of little avail on account of the great degree of fatness. The other method just mentioned [that is, putting the ear against the chest] being rendered inadmissible by the age and sex of the patient, I happened to recollect a simple and well-known fact in acoustics, and fancied it might be turned to some use on the present occasion. The fact I allude to is the great distinctness with which we hear the scratch of a pin at one end of a piece of wood, on applying our ear to the other. Immediately, on this suggestion, I rolled a quire [or sheaf] of paper into a kind of cylinder and applied one end of it to the region of the heart and the other to my ear, and was not a little surprised and pleased, to find that I could thereby perceive the action of the heart in a manner much more clear and distinct than I had ever been able to do by the immediate application of the ear.*

Laënnec knew he was onto something, and he pursued his discovery. He tried listening to the chest with longer and shorter coils of paper, with hollowed-out pieces of wood, with solid wood, and glass, and various metal cylinders. He even tried listening through a friend's oboe. Finding wood worked best, he varied the type, trying ebony, cedar, malacca cane, and limewood. He made these instruments himself, on a lathe, and called them stethoscopes, from the Greek word *stethos,* "chest," and Latin *-scopium,* referring to a means of observing. Finally he settled upon a foot-long cylinder of beechwood with a very narrow hole down the middle and scooped-out ends. He began manufacturing stethoscopes to be sold along with a book on how they were to be used.

All this work—his medical practice, his book writing, his stethoscope making, and his teaching as well—was done while Laënnec suffered from his own case of tuberculosis. Shortly before the book was to be released, he was overcome with exhaustion, and just as he was about to achieve glory and fame, he decided he could no longer manage his work, and left Paris for the more restful countryside. At the time his symptoms were not clearly those of tuberculosis: he felt very, very weak, and dizzy, and so depressed he hardly wanted to live, but he had no sure sign of what was killing him.

Laënnec continued to work strenuously whenever he could, and was forced to rest more than he desired, going for long stays in the country with his dogs Moustache and Kiss. Up until his death the cause of his illness was debated: even in his last months of life, when the doctors found an abdominal tumor, they wondered if that was the cause of all his symptoms. Laënnec wrote in his last letter that he had a patient once who was considered as hopeless as he but who had survived. Despite his optimism, Laënnec died the next Sunday, August 13, 1826, at the age of forty-five.

In fact, even if Laënnec could have heard in his lungs unmistakable sounds of the damage caused by tuberculosis, he could not have cured himself. Even seventy years later, after the discovery of X rays allowed tuberculosis to be spotted much earlier, medicine still had little to offer in the way of treatment or cure. Laënnec's life's work was merely one more step toward understanding the wiles of TB.

LUKE-SICK

For the most part, people like Laënnec who were sick with tuberculosis of the lungs felt a little sick for years, without being completely bedridden. For this reason, the disease was known as "consumption" or by the name the Greeks gave it, "phthisis," which means waning like the moon. During their long, slow decline, many sufferers, like Laënnec, went on to leave their mark on history. When the great American philosopher Ralph Waldo Emerson was just a divinity school student he wrote that he felt "luke-sick," as one might say "lukewarm," and as if a "mouse was gnawing at his chest." Emerson continued to suffer from symptoms of chronic tuberculosis throughout his life—although he lived to the age of seventy-nine. The philosopher Henry David Thoreau lived and worked with tuberculosis. A tubercular Chopin was still able to write his renowned music. And many writers had TB: Robert Louis Stevenson wrote *Treasure Island* and *Dr. Jekyll and Mr. Hyde,* and Stephen Crane wrote *The Red Badge of Courage,* while harboring *Mycobacterium tuberculosis.* The Brontë sisters suffered from tuberculosis, as did their whole family, but they managed to give the world the classic novels *Jane Eyre* and *Wuthering Heights.* One wonders what these people would have done if they had not been luke-sick.

In fact, so many brilliant young artists suffered from tuberculosis that people began to think that either genius made one susceptible to the disease or the disease itself gave one particular insight. In literature, characters with tuberculosis were likely to suffer as much from their passionate nature as from the disease. In the classic eighteenth-century Chinese novel *The Dream of the Red Chamber,* beautiful, young Black Jade dies of tuberculosis at the very moment her love is married to another woman.

In fact, a more likely reason passionate artists were dying was that tuberculosis was a disease of the city: the close contact between people that made the cities so stimulating for artists provided the perfect opportunity for the tuberculosis bacillus to travel from lung to lung. Droplets of TB germs exhaled out of doors could dry out before finding a lung, but in the crowded rooms of the city, people breathed in one another's breath again and again. And among the poor, who were continually overworked and underfed, tuberculosis found one vulnerable host after another. So it was that tuberculosis, which had infected humans for thousands of years, had its chance to flourish only when people lived in cities. When the Scottish explorer David Livingstone traveled through rural Africa in the mid-nineteenth century, he found very few people with tuberculosis. The same was true of Native Americans when Europeans first came to America. The disease was not unknown, the way smallpox was, but among fairly healthy people living in scattered small groups, like the Native Americans, tuberculosis did not flourish. But after Native Americans were moved to crowded reservations, it ran rampant. And today in African cities, larger and more crowded than anything Livingstone saw, tuberculosis is a leading killer, especially where there are large populations infected with Human Immunodeficiency Virus, or HIV, the virus that causes AIDS. HIV makes one especially vulnerable to TB.

In Japan, from 1910 to 1950, the growth of cities brought about a tuberculosis epidemic that was to be the country's worst experience with infectious disease this century. The stage for the epidemic was set at the turn of the century as the country's six largest cities—Tokyo, Yokohama, Nagoya, Osaka, Kyoto, and Kobe—swelled with people from the villages seeking work. They arrived from the countryside penniless and desperate for any kind of work to save them from the poverty they knew at home. Many found jobs in the Japanese silk and cotton industries. They stayed in crowded factory dorms and put in fifteen- or sixteen-hour days in crowded, unventilated factories. They were given no more than thirty minutes to eat and no time to wash before meals. As the workers slept and worked in shifts, their futons were never empty, their shared bedding never given time to air out. When tuberculosis found these factories, it thrived. When the workers got sick, as so many did, they were sent home. And when they returned to their villages, they spread the disease to their families.

The textile factories' reputation became so bad even people desperate for a job refused to work there. The factories were forced to send recruiters to more and more remote cities, and this helped spread the disease far and wide. A great epidemic began. Between 1910 and 1950 six million people were to die of tuberculosis in Japan, at a time when the country's population ranged from 50 to 93 million. By the end of these years, hardly a family in the entire nation was not touched by this disease.

SEAWEED, SAXOPHONES, AND MAGIC MOUNTAINS

For the six thousand years that we know people have had tuberculosis, it has been only during the past fifty that medical science could help them at all. However, even with no treatment, sometimes people got better on their own. This meant that over the years that they were ill, people might try something, such as Laënnec's seaweed treatment, and sometimes would happen to get better. But it was difficult to tell with a slow-moving disease whether a treatment really helped or only seemed to help.

Over the thousands of years of the history of tuberculosis, thousands of things have seemed to work. For a bloody cough, people have taken sulfur, garlic, quince, endive, cabbage, and burnt lungs of vulture mixed with lily blossoms and wine. For a cough, they have tried the herbs horehound and dill, boiled crocodile, and a lukewarm bath in urine taken from persons who had just eaten cabbage. Tuberculosis sufferers have ingested quinine, tea, coffee, cocoa, tobacco, cod-liver oil, and opium. They have been bled, blistered, and made to vomit. They have rubbed human fat on their tubercular necks. People have ingested twelve eggs a day, lobster, milk from highland goats, milk from asses, and milk from humans. They have been force-fed, and they have been starved. Some patients have been ordered to lie flat and still, forbidden even to so much as talk or laugh; others have been told to ride horseback six hours a day, to ski, to spin in revolving chairs until they were nauseous. Adolphe Sax, who invented the saxophone, claimed that playing wind instruments staved off consumption. Others swore swinging on a swing was the answer.

Kings and queens of France and England from the Middle Ages until the early nineteenth century laid their hands on people suffering from tuberculosis of the lymph nodes and were said to heal them. This type of tuberculosis infection, known as scrofula, causes the neck to swell in two great bulges below the corners of the jaw, and then open in foul-smelling sores. Left untreated, the disease could spread onto the face. Though not fatal, it was horribly disfiguring, and people would travel on foot from the farthest

I·WAS·IN·BED·TEN·HOURS— OR·MORE·LAST·NIGHT·AND· KEPT·MY·WINDOW·OPEN—

I·TOOK·TEN·OR·MORE·SLOW· DEEP·BREATHS·OF·FRESH— AIR·TO·DAY·

Fresh air came to be considered vital to preventing and curing tuberculosis, as promoted in these U.S. public health posters from the 1920s

corners of the kingdom to be touched by the King. Sometimes, on their weeks- or months-long journey back home, the scrofula went away, leading to the conclusion that the King's touch had healed them.

The most common treatment over the years was to move to a different climate. Some tuberculosis patients went to the seashore; others preferred the mountains. In Europe, patients went to the Mediterranean and to the Alps. In India, they went to the desert. In the United States, they went to Colorado, Minnesota, and the Arizona desert—some even moved into Kentucky's Mammoth Cave. Those who hadn't the strength to travel were given pillows of pine needles to sleep on or seaweed to put under their bed to mimic a mountain or seashore setting.

Toward the end of the nineteenth century, people who could afford it began to go to "sanatoriums" for treatment. The first were a cross between resort and hospital, inns in the mountains where people followed the latest cure fads, bundled up to rest outdoors for fresh air year round, and discussed their disease over lavish meals. The German novelist Thomas Mann based his classic novel *The Magic Mountain* on an alpine sanatorium in Davos, Switzerland, where patients gorged on five meals a day.

Edward Livingston Trudeau established the first American sanatorium at Saranac Lake in the Adirondacks. Trudeau first came to the Adirondacks as a healthy young man to hunt and fish in the wilderness. A few years later, having developed tuberculosis, he returned too weak to stand but determined to spend what few weeks he thought he had left to live in the beautiful woods where he had once felt so alive. The guides filled a canoe with pine boughs and pillows to make a soft place for him to lie down, and took him out hunting. By propping himself up on one arm, he was able to fire his gun, and on his first day he killed a deer. To his

Doctors in Paris in the late 1800s "treating" a tuberculosis patient by infusing her with the blood of a goat

own surprise, by the end of three months he was walking in the woods, was eating like a horse, and had gained fifteen pounds. Trudeau determined to stay in the woods and to build a sanatorium so that others could reap the benefits of a stay in a wild and beautiful place.

As time went on, sanatoriums became as much places to isolate the sick from the healthy as they were places of healing: they were for the poor as well as the rich, were less lavish, were not necessarily in beautiful places, and did not necessarily have good food.

Treatment for the most part consisted of a long isolated rest away from the healthy world.

Charlie Moses, who was seventeen when he left New York City for the Ray Brook Sanatorium upstate in 1920, wrote:

> *I spent probably the happiest eleven months of my life in that sana-torium. It was a place which opened my eyes to the world . . . My par-ents didn't come up for eleven months. Nobody, nobody came up because it was supposed to have been a secret. In those days, tuber-culosis was a disease which you were supposed to conceal. It was almost like a venereal disease is now. And when my mother used to send me "care" packages of food and gifts and she would meet one of her sisters living in the area and they would see her, they would ask, "Where are you taking this?" "I am taking this to Charlie," she would say. "He is in college."*

Cast out of the world of the healthy, tuberculosis patients cre-ated a world of their own in the sanatoriums. One young Ameri-can patient, Betty MacDonald, who was a thirty-year-old working single mother of two girls when she found out she had tubercu-losis, describes entering the sanatorium world:

> *Getting tuberculosis in the middle of your life is like starting down-town to do a lot of urgent errands and being hit by a bus. When you regain consciousness, you remember nothing about the urgent errands. You can't even remember where you were going. The impor-tant things now are the pain in your leg; the soreness in your back; what you will have for dinner; who is in the next bed.*

Patients could spend five, ten, even twenty years in a numbing routine of bed rest and meals. When first admitted to the sanatorium she calls "The Pines" in 1938, MacDonald had to spend every day lying down: that meant no reading, no talking, no laughing, no reaching too far out of bed to get things. Betty was informed sternly that her red hair would be a liability, as a redhead was likely to be vivacious and thus to have difficulty lying still and solemn. Not lying still, she was told, would lead to death. Things did get better: after three months at the Pines, if you showed improvement, you could go outside on the sleeping porch and lie still, bundled in blankets against the cold. MacDonald began to think that life in the sanatorium would "make dying seem like a lot of fun."

Because patients lived in sanatoriums, sharing their rooms with total strangers, for months and years of their lives, the sanatorium world brought out the prejudice in people, and separate hospitals were built for blacks and Native Americans to stay. Although it might have been hard for Betty MacDonald to imagine a worse place to spend the first years of her thirties, a young Lakota woman, Madonna Swan, wrote of a sanatorium stay that was even more dreadful and nearly deadly. Madonna Swan was just sixteen when she found she had tuberculosis. She had seen four schoolmates suddenly begin to cough blood and rapidly die from the disease. She knew all too well where the chest pains and cough that she shared with them would lead, but Madonna was sent to the doctor before it was too late, and he sent her to the "Sioux San."

That was in 1944. During the first two years Madonna Swan spent at the Sioux San, no patient left alive—no one even went out on leave: the only patients to leave were the dead. The patients were all dressed in striped uniforms, like prisoners. Meals were beans and cornmeal spotted with mouse droppings. The healthier patients spent the morning bathing the sicker ones, and they all

At the White Haven tuberculosis sanatorium in Pennsylvania, treatment consisted of one large meal daily plus all the milk and raw eggs one could eat and plenty of fresh air, no matter what the weather. On the day this photograph was taken in 1904, it was 16 degrees below zero

spent the afternoons from one to five lying on their beds with bean bags on their chests. Madonna's treatment consisted of four pounds of bean bags on the chest and one cup of cod-liver oil to drink daily. The bean bags were supposed to compress the lungs and suffocate the germs. After six years of this treatment, the doctor told Madonna he didn't think she would live three more months. Frail, dying, twenty-two-year-old Madonna determined that if she was to die, she would die at home. Then she plotted her escape. With the help of a nurse she had become friendly with and her fellow patients, Madonna sneaked out of the Sioux San alive.

Madonna's parents, determined to save their daughter, went to the office of the governor of South Dakota in person to request that she be allowed into the "white" sanatorium. So it was that after six years of the Sioux San, Madonna was admitted to a different hospital with better food and the best treatments available. First her lung was collapsed, in hopes of suffocating the germs. Then all her ribs on one side were removed: since she could hardly breathe, the bugs would get less oxygen. Once drugs that could kill tuberculosis were discovered, such treatments as these were abandoned—and as we look back, it is hard to imagine that they did any good—but at the time, with no other alternatives, doctors would try just about anything. Somehow, because of or despite these treatments, Madonna recovered.

As prisonlike as the Pines might have been for Betty MacDonald, as painful as Madonna Swan found her treatments, these two were considered among the lucky ones: they got into sanatoriums. Around the world, when sanatorium care was all the rage, there were not nearly enough sanatoriums for patients. In 1905 there were three times as many people on the waiting list at a Philadelphia sanatorium as there were beds. In India, by 1935, there was room in sanatoriums for only six thousand of the country's two and a half million patients. Even worse, it was not clear that sanatorium treatment, which was the only one available, was doing any good. Some better treatment was clearly needed, and soon.

BRILLIANT BLUE RODS

The first step to finding a treatment was to discover what caused the disease. That was no easy task. The slow-growing tuberculosis bug hid from scientists very well for so long because *Mycobacterium tuberculosis* has many tricks up its sleeve. First of all, it infects many different parts of the body. No one would suspect that a person with a swollen festering neck, one with a bloody cough, and one with a crooked spine were all suffering from the same disease. Even after a few brilliant doctors—Laënnec was one—saw through this ploy and began to suspect the germ was the same in all these cases, they still had to find it.

To make things even more difficult, some of the best minds in science were convinced that tuberculosis was not caused by a germ at all. Because it took years for infected people to show signs of illness, it was hard to connect the disease to exposure to a germ. A quick-moving disease such as plague or smallpox makes its contagiousness obvious: plague and smallpox could move through a household in a matter of days. But with tuberculosis, when Keats lived with his sick mother and breathed in tuberculosis germs, he remained healthy. It was years later that he became sick.

At the same time, there were those who nevertheless believed that tuberculosis was caused by a contagious agent, a bacterium. The end of the nineteenth century was a propitious time for these scientists. The day had come when they could develop the tools to find such very tiny creatures, even one as small and sly as tuberculosis. The lucky man who would find the tuberculosis bacillus was a young German country doctor named Robert Koch.

Koch was born in a small mining town, the third of thirteen children. Eleven of the children lived to adulthood, a good proportion at that time, when parents could expect infectious disease to kill several of their offspring. So many of Koch's brothers and sisters probably survived because their father was head of the mine and could afford the best of care. Little did anyone know that nearsighted Robert, who was his mother's favorite, was to bring to the world a means to fight the diseases that routinely killed so many children.

Koch grew up dreaming of adventure, of being a ship's doctor and traveling to unknown lands, but he also fell in love with his childhood sweetheart, Emmy Fraatz, and in the end gave up his dreams of travel to marry her and settle down as a small-town doctor. His mind never stopped its curious wanderings, however, and soon his home was a collection of specimens taken from the nearby ponds and marshes that he would examine under his microscope. He kept a menagerie of pigeons, dogs, chickens, cats, and foxes. He dabbled in the relatively new field of electrical science, giving patients small shocks to see if it would have a beneficial effect, and delighting his daughter's friends by making their hair stand on end. It was in 1875, after a tour of medical and scientific meetings, that he turned his thoughts to the question some

Robert Koch

of the best minds in Europe were pursuing: how to find microorganisms that caused disease.

Gerhard Hansen had isolated the germ he believed caused leprosy, but Koch not only would be the first to prove that a microorganism could cause disease, when, in 1876, he found the bug that caused the disease anthrax—a disease of farm animals that can be transmitted to humans—but also would establish the steps scientists have used ever since to show, beyond a doubt, that a particular tiny microscopic creature causes a particular illness. Some scientists had come to believe the way to prove a germ caused a disease would be to find the germ in the body of someone who was sick, take the germ out and grow it on its own outside the body, and then show that infecting another animal with the germ would cause the disease. Koch developed the methods that made this process possible, and found a way to ferret out even the elusive tuberculosis.

Tuberculosis proved especially difficult from step one. The first problem in tracking down a microorganism was to find a germ that is too small to see with the naked eye—when one does not even know what to look for. Even with a microscope, one needs to have a way of distinguishing the germ from the stuff it is living in. Eventually, the trick of staining the germs with a chemical that makes them a different color from that of the other tissue around them was discovered. Although this method allowed scientists to see most bacteria, tuberculosis had one more trick up its sleeve: the germ was encased in a thick waxy coat that was impervious to any stain. It was not until 1882 that Robert Koch found that when he stained bits of TB-infected lung with one particular old bottle of methylene blue dye that he had lying around his laboratory, and then washed them with a second, brown, stain, tiny bright blue rods appeared.

Koch was brilliant but he was also lucky. It was his luck that ammonia vapors had gotten into his old bottle of methylene blue. The ammonia mixed into the dye could eat through the bacillus's unique protective coating and allow the dye to get inside. It was by accident that Koch was able to see for the first time the creature that had been killing human beings for centuries. But Koch had no way of knowing that these were the germs he sought and not just some other bugs that happened to be in this lung. Could the rods be the cause of tuberculosis?

The next step would be to grow the rods outside the body. How does one grow bacteria? Scientists had been growing the bugs in pools of a liquid nutrient. One of Koch's favorites was the liquid from inside an ox's eye. But in a world swarming with microbes, it was hard to keep other bacteria out of these pools. They became a crowded mess of bugs, making it very difficult to infect another animal with one specific germ. In solving this problem, Koch would prove his brilliance. He considered the merits of a method that had been tried by some other researchers, who had grown bugs on the cut surface of a potato.

If you have ever found mold growing on solid foods in your refrigerator, you may have noticed that it grows in distinct patches, each with its own color and texture. Koch observed about this phenomenon:

> *What can we conclude from these observations of colonies developing on potatoes? . . . Most often each colony is a pure culture [all one type of microorganism] and remains a pure culture until it enlarges to the point that it touches its neighbors. If instead of the potato, a liquid medium . . . were exposed to the air, then undoubtedly the same number and the same kinds of germs would develop as on the potato, but the development of these germs in the liquid would be differ-*

ent . . . Some of the organisms would sink to the bottom of the liquid, while others would rise to the top . . . In short, the whole liquid would reveal under the microscope . . . a tangled mixture of different shapes and sizes.

Koch concluded that if he could make one of his excellent liquid bacteria foods solid, he would have the perfect solution. It was actually Frau Hesse, the wife of one of Koch's co-workers, who came up with the perfect way to make a solid culture medium: agar-agar, a gelatin-like substance derived from seaweed and used to harden jams, turned out to be such a perfect bacteria food it is still used today. It is solid at body temperature, the temperature disease-causing bacteria like best.

The first bug Koch grew on agar-agar was TB. It took patience: only after two long weeks of waiting and watching these seemingly empty plates did tiny waxy flakes appear. Very slowly, the flakes expanded. When Koch took and stained a flake and looked at it under the microscope, he again saw the brilliant blue bars. Even more amazing, if he took a flake and injected it into a guinea pig, the poor guinea pig came down with tuberculosis. Then, when Koch sacrificed the guinea pig for science and stained a little of its diseased tissue, he again found the tiny blue bars, which could then be taken and grown on the plates. Koch believed that this proved that the blue rods caused TB, but he did not want to be wrong. He conducted the experiment again and again. He injected a chicken, a cat, a pigeon, a mouse, a rat, an ox, and even a marmoset. Through this painstaking, methodical work, Koch convinced himself and then the world that he had found the cause of tuberculosis. Tuberculosis had been killing humans for centuries: in just eight months of study, Koch had discovered its cause.

After he had found the germ, Koch went on to discover a protein that led to a clever way to test if TB was in the body. Instead of doctors having to rely on finding evidence of TB's damage by stethoscope or even X ray, this method would reveal if one had merely breathed in the bacilli. How? A harmless protein that was part of the bacteria was injected just under the skin. If the immune system had seen TB before and so become armed against the disease, it would respond by sending battalions of warriors to the spot, raising a red circle under the skin as they swarmed in. On the other hand, if this protein was new to the body, the unarmed immune system would largely ignore it. This is the test your doctor still uses today to see if you have been exposed to TB. A positive test does not mean that you have TB, only that your body is armed against the disease. That could mean that you once breathed in the germ, fought it off for the time being, but may harbor some lingering bacilli that have a chance of one day causing disease. Your doctor can then X-ray your lungs to be sure you have no signs of active tuberculosis, and if you do, can treat you early, before the disease can take hold.

FROM THE THROAT OF A CHICKEN

However difficult a feat it was, finding the germ was not enough: sixty years after Koch's discovery of the tuberculosis germ, there was still no effective treatment for the disease. And then, sixty-one years after the germ's discovery, the world suddenly changed: two scientists in New Jersey found a drug that killed tuberculosis. Streptomycin it was called, and it emerged from the throat of a chicken.

Streptomycin was part of a revolution in medicine brought about by the discovery of drugs that could kill germs but not the people they infected. These drugs were to change the way we thought about disease. As recently as the 1930s, a simple cut that became infected could be a death sentence. The sore throat that killed George Washington in 1799 might still have been fatal. Then, in 1932, a German scientist named Gerhard Domagk discovered that a particular stain used by bacteriologists killed germs but did not seem to hurt humans. Before his drug was fully tested, Domagk's daughter developed an infection from a splinter she stabbed into her hand while sliding down a banister. Fearing the unknown drug less than the known infection, Domagk treated her with his new drug, and she survived. In the years to follow, hundreds of people were to write to Domagk to tell him how his drug had saved them from what would have been certain death. But Domagk's drug could not kill all types of germs. Everywhere scientists searched for others. And in New Jersey, Selman Waksman looked in the throat of a chicken.

Selman Waksman was a scientist who studied dirt at Rutgers University. What Waksman found in the throat of the chicken was a microbe that usually lived in the soil. People had observed for years that a tuberculosis germ placed in soil did not live for very long. They began to suspect that perhaps one of the microbes that lived in the dirt might kill tuberculosis germs. It made sense that in the tiny microbe world, just as among the larger creatures on the earth, there would be competition for space and food, and the microbes might be drawn into fighting one another. Perhaps some of the soil microbes had ways to kill tuberculosis that could even be used as a drug.

Selman Waksman had been studying soil microbes since the time he was in college. In the early thirties he did some experiments to see what he could learn about soil microbes and TB. He took some soil, treated it so all the microbes were killed, and then put some tuberculosis germs in it. Instead of quickly dying, as TB did in dirt with living microbes, the TB germs in the sterilized dirt lived happily. It seemed that some microbe was doing the killing. But it was not until years later that Waksman, working with a graduate student named Albert Schatz, was to find the bug that did it.

In the summer of 1943, a New Jersey farmer found that one of his chickens was having trouble breathing. Fearing a disease that might infect all of his flock, the farmer brought the chicken in for testing at a laboratory that specialized in tracking agricultural diseases. One of Waksman's assistants was working in the lab that examined a swab from this chicken's throat. When he saw that one of the bugs found in the chicken's throat was one of Waksman's favorite soil microbes, *Streptomyces,* he saved the specimens for Waksman. Albert Schatz, the graduate student, had audaciously pledged to discover a cure for tuberculosis for his graduate research. He took the microbes, grew many more of them, and began to test all their excretions to see if one killed tuberculosis. In fact, one did. He named the drug made from this excretion after the microbes it came from.

In November of 1944, Patricia, a twenty-one-year-old woman who was dying of tuberculosis, was started on a course of streptomycin, and by the following April she was cured. Patricia, who would have died, went on to have three children. She could be your grandmother. For the thousands of people in sanatoriums waiting to die, it was a miracle, a true new lease on life. The bloody cough was no longer a death sentence.

Streptomycin was among the first of many microbial weapons to be sold as a drug. As we have seen, it was also an effective plague killer. These drugs produced by microbes became known as the antibiotics, and they turned the tables in the fight against infectious disease, for a while at least. In rapid succession, several more drugs were found that could fight tuberculosis. Patients greeted the discovery of these drugs by dancing in the halls of the sanatoriums. The news was spectacular: those formerly too thin and weak to walk were up and wandering the halls; an old man who could hardly be forced to eat was now demanding eleven eggs for breakfast. In 1954, the Trudeau Sanatorium at Saranac was closed, an event that seemed to mean the end of an era, that tuberculosis would be no more. In the exhilaration, it was hard to pay attention to the uncomfortable truth that tuberculosis was not to be so easily defeated, that this disease had at least one more trick up its sleeve.

OUTLASTING THE DRUGS

Soon after streptomycin's glorious discovery, a troubling thing occurred. When some patients took the drug, they felt much better for the first couple of months: they gained weight, and the tuberculosis bugs they coughed up had been killed by the drug. Then, strangely, the drug stopped working, the coughing and weakness returned, and the bugs they coughed up were alive and kicking and no amount of streptomycin could kill them. With no other cure possible, these patients could go on to die, and anyone infected by their hardy germs could not be treated by streptomycin either. It appeared that tuberculosis was learning how to outsmart the drug!

Of course, tuberculosis is just a bacterium; it does not have a brain in its tiny rod-shaped body. It cannot learn anything, so how was it getting around streptomycin? The answer is this: drug-resistant strains were evolving. A person infected with tuberculosis is like an island nation of TB germs. When assaulted by an antibiotic, all the germs begin to die. However, in this nation, there might be some germs that are just a little different, as there are people in any crowd who are just a little different. These germs might be different in a way that makes them able to withstand streptomycin's assault. During drug treatment, as all the normal

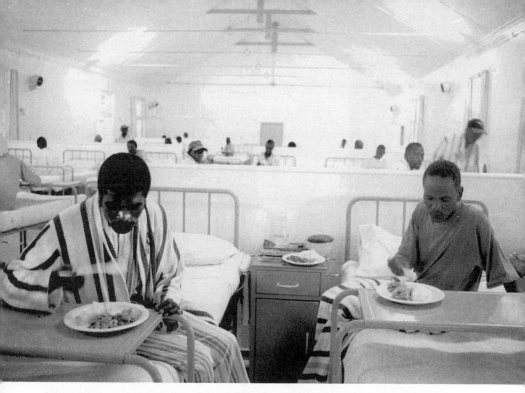

South Africa today has the world's highest rate of tuberculosis infection and lacks proper facilities for treatment. In this Johannesburg hospital, patients with a drug-resistant form of the disease share the same room as patients who have the treatable disease and could easily catch the more severe form

TB germs were killed, the abnormal strain would survive, with more room to grow and more food to eat because all the normal bugs were dead. After a few months, the abnormal germs would have filled the whole body with their drug-resistant offspring.

Doctors found they could overcome drug resistance if they gave patients several drugs at once: it was much rarer for bacilli to outwit three drugs at the same time, and if people with tuberculosis took the drugs long enough, for six months to a year, so few bacilli had a chance to survive that they were not a threat. Once more than one drug to fight tuberculosis was found, it seemed that this could be a solution. But there is another problem. Multidrug therapy seems to clear up tuberculosis rather quickly, relieving symptoms in a matter of weeks. Meanwhile, among these bacilli might be one that was weird enough to resist two of the three drugs. If bombarded long enough with all three, even this germ will die. But patients do not know about this bacillus. What they know is that the strong drugs make them feel sick. So, out of discomfort—or forgetfulness, or poverty—people stop taking the drugs too soon. When they do, the weird TB germ has a chance to reproduce. Among its offspring could be an even weirder bug unable to be killed by any of the drugs being used. This has happened so many times there are now some strains of TB that are resistant to seven drugs.

It has been this ability to develop resistance, as well as tuberculosis's preference for attacking people when their defenses are down, that has led to a resurgence of tuberculosis just when we thought we had it defeated. In the United States, between 1953 and 1987 the overall number of tuberculosis cases declined by 73 percent. At the same time, however, among minorities in the United States, who were more likely to be poor, the decline was not nearly so steep, and in some developing countries rates were not falling at all. The discovery of an effective cure for tuberculosis was not enough. We still needed to get the drugs to people and to get them to take the drugs for the full six months or more necessary to be cured. Taking the expensive drugs for six months was especially difficult for the poor. Public funds were needed to get the drugs to people. However, as tuberculosis declined among many people, it seemed less and less important to spend money on it. In New York City, in the ten years between 1968 and 1978, the money spent to fight tuberculosis dropped by half.

It was in 1979 that the number of cases of tuberculosis in New York City began to rise again. By 1987, they had increased by 45 percent. New York had the largest increase of tuberculosis in the country, but nationwide rates also increased, as they did in much of Western Europe.

There were three reasons that tuberculosis began to thrive while public agencies slept. One was the difficulty of taking the drugs for so long. In New York City, a sharp rise in homelessness increased this problem. Not only were the homeless vulnerable to contracting tuberculosis in crowded shelters, but their unstable living arrangements and poverty made it especially difficult to follow a complicated drug regimen. This already difficult situation was made much worse by the worldwide spread of the human immunodeficiency virus, or HIV, the virus that causes AIDS. An HIV-weakened immune system was less able to arm the macrophages to kill off new tuberculosis infections and also had a hard time keeping old dormant infections in check. Around the world, wherever HIV infection rates were high, tuberculosis rates began to soar. By the year 2000, it is estimated, there will be fifteen million new cases of tuberculosis in Africa south of the Sahara.

Today, New York City is one of the few places in the world that has actually turned around its tuberculosis epidemic: since 1993 rates of tuberculosis infection have dropped there. The key to beating back tuberculosis has been a program known as Directly Observed Therapy Short-Course, or DOTS, which means having someone watch while patients take their tuberculosis drugs. Imagine thousands of people with tuberculosis scattered across New York City being tracked down and watched every day while they swallow their pills. This is time-consuming and expensive, but it works, and not just in New York. In Africa, the countries of Benin, Malawi, and Tanzania now cure more than 80 percent of cases of the disease by using DOTS, as do Chile and Honduras in the Americas. In Asia, home to two thirds of people suffering from tuberculosis, DOTS programs have been instituted in China, South Korea, Malaysia, and Vietnam. Where DOTS has been tried in India, 80 percent of people are cured. Unfortunately, more than three quarters of the people in this populous nation remain without a DOTS program, and HIV infection rates are climbing. Throughout the world, fifty thousand people will die this week of tuberculosis.

What do we need to fight TB? The best answer we have today seems to be DOTS. And what do we need to do DOTS? Money. WHO predicts that if about $100 million more dollars a year is spent on tuberculosis programs worldwide in the next ten years, twelve million lives will be saved. Without increased funding, by the year 2006, the number of people who die each year of tuberculosis will increase by one million, an additional three thousand deaths a day. Tuberculosis is a disease that will not fade into the past.

MALARIA

THE UNBEATABLE TEAM
OF PARASITE AND MOSQUITO

The three men rushed along the dirt path as fast as they could. One glanced over his shoulder at the sun turning orange on the horizon. They raced against this setting sun: if they were not within their little cottage by the light of its last rays, their experiment would be useless, and, if they believed the man who had sent them to this damp town, they could be doomed to the fevers and chills of malaria!

These three, two English doctors and an Italian artist, had been living here, in the marshy lands outside Rome known as the Roman Campagna, for fifty-two days now, since the beginning of July, in the year 1900. This was a place that for hundreds of years had given to its inhabitants, and to those who dared to visit, the burning fevers and racking chills that had come to be called malaria. Malaria—from the words *mala,* "bad," and *aria,* "air," was the name Italians had given this disease when they were convinced that it rose from the stinking air of these Campagna swamps. Now these men had been sent to live in this damp place among its fever-stricken farmers to prove that malaria came not

Long before the malaria parasite was discovered inside a mosquito, insects were suspected of causing disease, as suggested by this image from the *Hortus Sanitatis,* a widely read medical book from 1491

from the swamp air they had been breathing for fifty-two days, nor from the water everyone drank in this place, but from the bites of mosquitoes. And not just any mosquitoes, but only one type, the female *Anopheles*, a mosquito that took its meal of blood only at night. They sought to prove that a germ that lived inside the *Anopheles* and entered humans through the insect's blood-sucking bite was the cause of malaria.

Malaria has plagued men and women as long as they have walked on the earth. When they settled in their earliest civilizations in the moist river valleys of Mesopotamia and the lands that would become India and China, malaria was there with its terrible fevers. For centuries people thought of swamps as unhealthy places, but only a few over the course of history thought that the mosquitoes humming in the humid air might be the source of the disease. Even after 1897, when an Englishman working in India, Ronald Ross, found the parasite that caused malaria in the stomach of the *Anopheles* mosquito, people remained unconvinced. So in 1900 Patrick Manson, Ross's mentor, who had believed for fourteen years that mosquitoes carried malaria, sent these three men to live in this malarious swamp to prove it to the doubting public by risking their very lives.

The germ that causes all this suffering has struck a bargain with the mosquito. It is a parasite, a creature that lives off another. The malaria parasite, known as *Plasmodium*, cannot complete its life cycle without living part-time in this mosquito and part-time in a human being. The female *Anopheles*—a name that means "harmful"—cannot produce a fertile egg without a drink of blood. It is the perfect marriage, this match of parasite and mosquito. The *Anopheles'* one-month life span is just long enough for the parasites to mature in the mosquito's stomach and be ready to infect a person. The *Anopheles* bites a malaria-infected

A spirit rising from the marshes sickens the people of humid Berry, France, as painted by Maurice Sand in the mid-nineteenth century

human and sucks up parasites in its drink of blood, the parasites mature, and the *Anopheles* spits them back out into someone else.

Because the parasite so depends on the *Anopheles,* the story of malaria is the story of how, together, this tiny team has stopped so many humans in their tracks. The Goths sacking Rome, African highlanders moving down to the coast of what is now Tanzania, Europeans exploring Africa, and settlers moving into the Mississippi and Ohio valleys—all have found their ways made deadly by malaria. And this perfect marriage of mosquito and parasite has made malaria a very difficult disease to fight. Today about four hundred million people have malaria and about two to three million will die this year, most of them children in Africa. Of all infectious diseases, only tuberculosis will kill more. All these people still die from malaria even after, in the 1950s and '60s, hundreds of millions of dollars was spent on an unsuccessful plan to eradicate the disease from the planet.

THE GRAVE OF GRAVES

Outside the walls of Rome, center of the ancient empire that was to leave a lasting legacy, stretched a vast, remarkable wasteland called the Campagna. Although in its midst a city was to arise to dominate the Western world for centuries, this land again and again returned to desolation. The Roman Empire, which could overcome most of Europe, could do little to civilize its Campagna. Some force was at work there that was equal even to the force of empire.

Over the years people tried to cultivate the area surrounding Rome. The fertile, flat lands that extended as far as the eye could see could be used to grow food for the city dwellers. The wealthy men who owned the land were asked to tend and plant their estates. Nevertheless, they let them go to waste. The land itself was unhealthy, they claimed: despite the fertility of its soil, those who worked its fields were doomed to fall ill and die.

The Campagna's legendary murderousness was recorded by Roman poets: Virgil wrote that "our youth were busy with marriages and new tillage [when] on a sudden from a tainted quarter of the sky, came a pestilence and season of death." The fever was worst in the fall, darkening the joy of harvesttime: it became "death-bearing autumn" when "every father and fond mother turns pale with fear for the children." They feared fierce intermittent fevers. These high fevers with racking chills came in regular cycles, every few days. First came chills that set the sufferers' teeth chattering. For nearly an hour they would shake so hard their bodies rattled their beds. Then their temperature began to rise. They threw off the blankets they had been clutching to their chin, their pinched faces turned red with heat, and they begged for water. Only after two hours of this dry, hot agony did they begin to sweat. As the moisture ran down their faces, their foreheads cooled and they fell asleep. When they awoke, they would be fine for two to three days until it all began again.

At the time of the Romans, no one knew why this land was so deadly. Many suspected it had to do with the wetness of the soil: people who lived in swamps got sick and died. The Greeks had a saying about the town Sybaris, which lay in a hot moist valley in southern Italy: "He who does not wish to die young must neither see the sun rise nor see it set in Sybaris." And Varro, writing in Rome in the first century B.C., warned:

> Precautions must also be taken in the vicinity of swamps . . . because there are bred certain minute creatures which the eyes are not able to detect and which pass from the air into the body through the mouth and nostrils and cause serious diseases.

The passage goes on to recommend that if you inherit swampy land and cannot sell it, you should abandon it.

Swampy earth even smelled unhealthy. Rotting vegetation in swamps released such repulsive rotten-egg-scented gases, and spookily glowing phosphorescent fumes, that it seemed completely possible that this foul air was unhealthy to breathe. If it wasn't the gases themselves, then maybe it was tiny unhealthy creatures that gave this air its stink and that rode these noxious vapors into your body, bringing with them the fever.

Mysteriously, these swampy lands and their disease-causing gases, which people came to refer to as miasmas, were even more deadly to visitors than to their inhabitants. Invaders, explorers, and new settlers were to find that the *mal' aria* was a watchdog.

In this British cartoon of 1792, a malaria victim shivers in the clawlike grip of the chills, while the fiery demon fever waits its turn. At the right, a doctor prepares a remedy

Pioneer settlers who moved out into the midwestern United States less than two hundred years ago found the humid and fertile river valleys of the Mississippi and the Ohio the source of this same fever. As fertile as the land might be, the settler who ignored the warnings and built his home there might soon find himself shaking and burning from malaria. A man named Timothy Flint wrote in 1832 of the dangers of the Mississippi valley: "A great portion of the immigrants to the western country have fixed themselves in open cabins that drink in the humid atmosphere of the night, through a hundred crevices, in a new and untried climate . . . Need we wonder that the country has acquired a general character of unhealthiness?"

Europeans ventured into the humid tropics at great peril. European slave traders who sailed to West Africa, then on to the New World before returning to Europe, had a one-in-five chance that they would be dead before the voyage ended. And the lives of those who explored the African continent were at even greater risk. Out of 281 persons taking part in six British expeditions in West Africa in the early nineteenth century, half were to die, most of malaria and yellow fever, another mosquito-carried disease. In 1806 the Scottish explorer Mungo Park, on his second, fatal, expedition to chart the course of the Niger River, wrote in his last letter, before drowning during an attack by hostile natives: "I am sorry to say that of forty-five Europeans who left the Gambia in perfect health five only are at present alive, namely three soldiers (one deranged in mind), Lieutenant Marty, and myself." Decades later, when it was clear malaria was spread by mosquitoes, this insect was thanked by at least one African for holding European colonists and explorers at bay. A lecturer at a university in the African country of the Ivory Coast is said to have suggested, "Let us give thanks therefore to that little insect the mosquito, which has saved the land of our fathers for us . . . The least we can do is engrave its picture on our national flag."

By 1900, when our three visitors were staying in the Campagna, the deadliness of swamps, especially to visitors, had been well confirmed by countless illnesses and deaths over thousands of years. Previous English visitors to Italy had described the Campagna as a "grave of graves," as a desolate land, whose few residents were "of a cadaverous hue, wretched and ragged." For visitors, the evening miasma was considered so pernicious that passengers on the train to Rome who passed through the Campagna during these hours pulled up their windows despite the heat. And to stay a night in the place was simply considered fatal.

So you can imagine the thoughts that went through the minds of our three experimenters as they lay at night in their Campagna hut, with only thin screens, through which the night air blew freely, between them and this desolate land. The man who had sent them was safely back in London, where the breeze could not reach. Could they believe, as he did, that the death and destruction of this place were the result of the bite of one tiny insect?

THE BARK THAT STILLED MALARIA'S BITE

Just as the European explorers in Africa and the settlers in North America were ravaged by malaria, so were the Spanish colonists in the jungles of Peru. It was the Peruvian Indians who were to introduce these suffering colonists to perhaps the most valuable medication the human race has ever known. Long before anyone suspected a parasite of causing the disease, Peruvian Indians had found a source of relief from its terrible fevers.

Bark from a tree that grew in the Peruvian forest was to save so many lives that legends have developed about its origin. Some say that the beautiful young wife of a Spanish count, who was a viceroy in Lima at the time, was stricken by a terrible case of intermittent malarial fever. The count was terrified that she would die and desperate for something to save her, when someone suggested that he try the bark of the fever tree. So the countess was given an infusion, or tea, made of this bark; her fever receded, and she lived. When she recovered, she distributed the bark to all the Spanish colonists in Lima so that they might be saved from the terrible fevers, and then the countess brought it back to Europe.

The only problem with this romantic story is that in the count's diary, which has recently been found, there is no mention at all of his wife having a fever or even being sick. It appears that his wife was unusually healthy while she was in Peru, but that she died on her return trip to Spain. It is not clear how the fever-tree bark made it back to Spain, but it seems unlikely that the countess had anything to do with it.

The best guess of historians is that Jesuit missionaries in Peru learned the use of the bark from the Indians. Although the written evidence is slim, some Spanish colonists recorded that the Indians who lived near a place called Loxa, high in the Andes mountains where the fever tree grew, used its bitter bark to treat their fevers.

It is very likely that the Indians knew of the use of this bark: their pharmacy was the forest, and their healers prescribed plants. Many Spanish explorers and colonists wrote with awe of the Indians' knowledge of using plants for medicine. Of just one plant, for instance, the Indians knew to use the young tender branches to clean their teeth, a tea of the leaves for skin diseases, the resin as a laxative, and the bark to reduce swelling. It has been said that Spanish soldiers would rather have native healers than Spanish doctors treat their wounds. Fever-tree bark was only one of many barks, resins, and herbs sent back from the New World to the Old as newfound cures. Although we do not know for sure how it happened, it is likely that some Peruvian healer once led a Jesuit missionary to the fever tree, sharing its age-old secret.

The bark and stories of its powers eventually found their way across the Atlantic to Rome in the mid-seventeenth century, and to the Jesuit Cardinal de Lugo, who decided to see for himself what this drug could do. The cardinal had the Pope's personal physician try the drug on some people with fever to see if its acclaim as a cure was true. The cardinal was not disappointed. He was so impressed by the bark's effectiveness that he went on to use his own money to buy great quantities and to distribute it from his home free to the "fevered poor." He asked only that they promise to take the drug, not sell it, and that they first present a physician's note saying they suffered intermittent fevers, malaria's chief symptom.

It was important that the people who used the bark not be suffering from some other kind of fever: the drug worked only against malaria. Unfortunately, some physicians misdiagnosed their patients. This led to a great deal of controversy over whether or not the drug was effective: those who thought they had malaria but who actually had some other illness used the bark and did not improve. This was just one of the many reasons why it took years for people to become convinced that the bark really cured malaria.

Another problem that made people continually question the bark was the variation in its quality. Obtaining the bark was a long and arduous process. The fever tree could not grow in Europe: the bark had to be cut in autumn from trees high in the Andes and transported by foot and hoof hundreds of miles out of the rugged highlands to a coastal port. From there it had to travel up the west coast of South America to the isthmus of Panama, and then, provided it reached Panama before the drenching rainy season curtailed overland travel, it was carried across the isthmus to be shipped across the Atlantic. With luck, the trip could take a year. Along the way pirates and plunderers waited to seize the precious bark. The bark became very valuable and the riches to be made prompted all kinds of intrigue: dishonest people tried to sell the bark from other trees as fever-tree bark. Some of the mix-up was genuine: many were not sure which tree was in fact the fever tree. Between the counterfeit and the simply mistaken, there was a lot of bark in Europe that did nothing for a malarial fever.

On top of all that, even if they did get the real thing, people often had no idea how much to take or how often. It was not until 1820 that two French chemists determined which chemical in the bark was beneficial. Until that time, people could only measure how much of the bark they took. They did not know how much of the helpful chemical, known as quinine, was in a particular batch of bark.

For fifty years or so, even after the cardinal's tests, a debate raged in Europe over the efficacy of the bark. It didn't help that

The "tree of fevers" from a 1712 Italian medical book. The names in the branches with leaves are all names for malarial fevers that can be treated with fever-tree bark

Catholics were promoting its use: in Protestant countries in Europe it was condemned as "Jesuits' bark." But certainly over the years it became well enough respected as a remedy not only for pirates and counterfeiters to profit by it but also for it to be considered a gift fit for royalty. The empress of Hungary, Pope Clement XIV, the duke of Parma, and the electress of Bavaria were all presented with batches of bark as gifts.

The value of fever-tree bark only increased when people realized that the bark actually prevented fevers. We still do not understand exactly how quinine cures malaria or how it prevents the disease, but it became clear that if people took regular infusions of the drug, they did not get malaria. This discovery seems important enough for someone to have preserved its story, but all we know are snippets that we can try to piece together.

We know that the writer of one medical book in the mid-eighteenth century recorded how Europeans sailing to West Africa would take along the bark in order to grind it into a powder and mix it into wine for sailors to drink when they went ashore. We also know of one crew that accidentally became an experiment: in 1826 twenty members of the crew of a British ship, the HMS *North Star*, were sent ashore in Sierra Leone. All but one, Lieutenant Boultbee, drank daily infusions of the bark in wine. Boultbee, who was in charge of the group, did not take the drug he ordered everyone else to swallow, and he alone developed a raging fever.

We know the explorer David Livingstone took quinine in Africa in the 1850s. And we know that by 1844 one Dr. Sappington could sell enough quinine-containing "Anti-Fever Pills" in the southern United States to become a wealthy man. His advertisements were his twenty-five salesmen who, going door-to-door in the malaria-stricken South, took his pills and were never sick. Eventually, British people living in India found a way to make a "tonic" water from their bitter quinine that they drank with gin, thus inventing the gin and tonic. So from out of the Peruvian forest came a bark destined to be a gift for kings, the cure of millions, and the basis of a cocktail.

MALARIA'S BARGAIN

By living in the mosquitoes of a particular place, malaria reigned over it: most everyone who lived there got malaria. A disease that is always present in this way is known as an endemic disease. A person who lives in an area where malaria is endemic can become a teeming metropolis for *Plasmodium*. One researcher who examined Nigerians for parasites in 1930 found that by the time they were four months old, half of the children had malaria parasites in their blood, as did every single one of the one- and two-year-olds he examined. But malaria made a deal with the people it infected again and again since birth. People who survived their first five years without dying lived with malaria parasites swimming happily through them, reproducing, being sucked back out by new mosquitoes, and giving birth to more parasites within them. Except during a woman's first pregnancy, when for mysterious reasons malaria can again be deadly, for the rest of their lives most residents of malarious regions who were continually reinfected with the parasite suffered only the occasional fever and chill. Although these were disruptive, they were not life-threatening. As long as malaria did not kill these people, the parasite had a good thing going: it had a place to feed and breed.

If someone new should come into the region, someone whose blood had never known a malaria parasite, and this person was bitten by an infected mosquito—that was something else. Malaria can kill such newly exposed people.

Malaria comes in four varieties, each caused by a slightly different parasite, and each distinguished by both the frequency and recurrence of the fevers it brings, and their deadliness. When malaria first enters the human body, it goes to the liver and there transforms itself into a form that infects red blood cells. Malaria then moves into the red blood cells, dines on their hemoglobin—the molecule that carries oxygen—and reproduces until the blood cells burst. It is the bursting of the red blood cells that causes the racking chills and fever.

This cycle of infection occurs again and again, in some forms every two days, in others every three. Sometimes this goes on for months, but most often, if the host is a healthy adult and lucky, the infection is overcome—but not always forever. There are two forms of malaria in which some parasites linger in the liver for years and can without warning burst out again and again into rounds of fever-inducing infection. These recurrent infections, while infreqently deadly, drastically interrupt a person's life and work.

There is one last form of malaria, known as *Plasmodium falciparum*, which does not recur but is especially deadly. It is not the fever that is fatal: *P. falciparum* clogs tiny capillaries and shuts off the blood supply to vital organs. When it blocks blood vessels in the brain, or in the kidneys, the parasite can kill. Or it can interfere with the function of the lungs, causing them to fill up with fluid: the host drowns. People who live in a malarious area that is infected with *P. falciparum* can still become immune to its deadly effects, but it is especially deadly for the young, the pregnant, and the newcomer.

Some people in malarial parts of the world are born with special ways to resist malaria, in addition to the protection bestowed by repeated infections. These special forms of immunity have been developed over the millennia by the bodies of people living in areas with great numbers of the parasite. One of these protections is the sickle-cell trait. Individuals with this trait produce a special type of hemoglobin, causing their red blood cells to be inhospitable for the *P. falciparum* malaria parasite. If one of the parents of a child passes on this ability, the child is more likely to survive an early infection with malaria.

In Africa, where so many children get malaria, people with the sickle-cell trait are more likely to survive than those without. This is part of the reason why some African slaves in the southern United States suffered less from malaria than their white owners and overseers. If two people carrying the trait have children, however, then one in four of their offspring is likely to suffer from sickle-cell anemia. For the three million Americans of African descent who carry this trait and live far from any malaria-carrying mosquito, there is no advantage to the trait, only the risk of having children who suffer from this other dangerous disease.

ONE THOUSAND MOSQUITO STOMACHS LATER

By the time Ronald Ross, the Englishman who was to discover the malaria parasite, was born, in 1857, malaria was becoming a faint memory in England. The very last case of malaria on English soil occurred during his medical school days. Long before anyone attempted to eradicate it, malaria had begun to recede from Europe and North America. Although in the early 1700s malaria occurred as far north as Maine and Vermont in the American colonies, and as far north as Scandinavia in Europe, by the end of the century it had begun to disappear from northern Europe and America both. Why? Because of the way farmers changed the land.

Some types of agriculture encouraged malaria: in Portugal and South Carolina, for instance, when farmers flooded the land to grow rice, malaria moved right in. Clearing forests for cocoa farms in Africa also created a perfect home for the African *Anopheles*. But in New England and northern Europe, when farmers drained marshes to plant fields and kept the cattle they raised in barns, malaria began to disappear. The draining of marshes left mosquitoes without a home, and the few that remained were a type of *Anopheles* that preferred cows to humans, so they fed on the cows and stayed out of the farmhouses.

Without realizing it, farmers in northern North America and Europe had driven away malaria long before anyone even knew where the disease came from. But although malaria might have been leaving Europe, so were the Europeans. They were heading out to claim and rule lands throughout the tropics, where they caught malaria. So it was that Ross was born, not in cool, clammy England, but in the heat of India, the son of a British army officer, and it was to the heat of India that he would return to conduct the work on malaria that would win him the Nobel Prize.

Ross never wanted to be a doctor, much less a researcher. He wanted to write plays and poems, and to paint, and to be a composer and a mathematician. He did all that, but his father wanted him to be a doctor, so Ross halfheartedly found his way through medical school, to a post with the medical service treating British soldiers and colonists in India. But as halfhearted as Ross could be about medicine, when he did take an interest in something he attacked it with enthusiasm and nearly arrogant ambition. And when he heard the claim that a Frenchman named Charles Louis Alphonse Laveran had found tiny creatures swimming in the blood of his colonial malaria patients and was now claiming that this crea-

Ronald Ross and his portable microscope in India in 1898

ture caused the disease, Ross was interested. He looked for himself. He saw concave, red-rimmed disks of red blood cells, but no sign of the wriggling filaments, supposedly like tiny tentacles, that Laveran had claimed to see moving among the cells. Ross's interest turned into enthusiastic indignation, and he wrote articles announcing to the scientific community that in his opinion, there was no parasite in the blood, that malaria, in fact, was a disease of the intestines.

These were words Ross would live to regret. Just one year later, he found himself in London staring through the lens of a microscope at the very swirling creatures he had announced to the world did not exist. At least Ross had the humility and wisdom to visit an eminent scientist in London, Patrick Manson, who showed him the creatures.

Ross was not the only one to doubt Laveran, who had discovered a microbe that was very hard to find. Many people looked for the parasite in dried blood, where the parasite was impossible to see. Even in fresh blood, it usually appeared only as a pale round patch inside the red blood cell. For years, the inept who could not find the parasite called believing in the parasite "Laveranity," as if it were a form of insanity.

Although Patrick Manson worked in London, he had access to the Seaman's Hospital, where sailors regularly returned from the tropics full of fresh malarial blood for him to examine. And Manson had studied a disease called filariasis, a disease caused by a worm that was carried by mosquitoes. Manson was convinced that malaria worked the same way, but there in London, he had no mosquitoes to study.

Then along came Ross. Once Ross had seen the parasite himself, he became a passionate believer. And Manson encouraged him, believing that Ross had the perfect opportunity to prove to the world that the creature was carried by mosquitoes. Ross burned with enthusiasm. He invented a portable microscope and got started right away: aboard ship on his return trip to India, he dissected cockroaches because they had parasites he thought resembled *Plasmodium*.

Ross's task was to catch mosquitoes, feed them on malarial patients, cut them open, and look inside for malaria parasites. He sat in a small dark office in Secunderabad, India, dissecting mosquitoes from 7 a.m. until dusk. It was so hot the sweat from his forehead rusted his microscope. And, unfortunately, he knew nothing about mosquitoes. His servant brought Ross one thousand mosquitoes and he dissected each one meticulously, never realizing that none was the malaria-carrying type. Of the 2,500 species of mosquitoes known, only about 50 are forms of *Anopheles*.

It was not until August 16, 1897, when a dozen dapple-winged mosquitoes that had a habit of sitting with their hind end sticking up in the air were brought to him, that Ross hit the jackpot. They were placed under a mosquito net with his servant and chief mosquito feeder, the malaria-infected Husein Khan, until they had time to bite him. (Husein Khan was paid one anna for every bite, about enough money to buy a quarter pound of rice.) Over the next three days Ross dissected the dapple-wings, but he found nothing very intriguing other than a strange dark bulge in one's stomach. He was disappointed that these new mosquitoes had no surprise for him. On the fourth day, when he went to dissect one of the two that remained, he was so discouraged that at first he nearly gave up. He wrote of that day in his memoirs:

> The dissection was excellent and I went carefully through the tissues now so familiar to me, searching every micron with the same passion and care as one would search some vast ruined palace for a little hidden treasure. Nothing. No, these new mosquitoes also were going to be a failure: there was something wrong with the theory. But the stomach tissue still remained—lying there, empty and flaccid, before

me on the glass slide, a great white expanse of cells like a large court-
yard of flagstones, each one of which must be scrutinized—half an
hour's labour at least. I was tired, and what was the use? I must have
examined the stomachs of a thousand mosquitoes by this time.

Yet the discouraged Ross pressed on, and as his tired eye passed
over the even rows of cells that he knew so well, he was startled by
the appearance of circular cells unlike any he had seen before in
the stomach of a mosquito. Each was filled with a dark, grainy
stuff that very much resembled the pigment he had seen inside
Plasmodium! Ross remembered thinking, "If these cells were the
parasites, they should grow in size in the last remaining mosquito
during the night." He was so excited over his discovery, and so
frightened that the final dapple-wing would die before he had a
chance to dissect it, he could barely sleep that night. The next
morning he found that not only did the last mosquito contain
similar cells but they were bigger. Ross concluded they had grown.
He had found the parasite living and growing within the
mosquito! Ross the poet wrote:

> *This day relenting God*
> *Hath placed within my hand*
> *A wondrous thing; and God*
> *Be praised. At His command,*
>
> *Seeking His secret deeds*
> *With tears and toiling breath,*
> *I find thy cunning seeds*
> *O million-murdering Death.*
>
> *I know that this little thing*
> *A myriad men will save—*

O Death, where is thy sting?
Thy victory, O grave?

From that day on, Ross celebrated August 20 as "Mosquito Day."

SWATTING AT THE MOSQUITO

Within two years an Italian scientist, Giovanni Battista Grassi, who knew much more about mosquitoes than Ronald Ross, had proved that *Anopheles* and only *Anopheles* could carry malaria. But it took far more than the work of these two men to convince enough people that mosquitoes carried malaria. For that reason, Patrick Manson sent our three friends to the Campagna in 1900 to prove it with their lives. And just in case their screened survival was not convincing, Manson had *Anopheles* mosquitoes that had been fed on the blood of malarial Italian patients packaged in special net cages and sent to England. Then he let these parasite-filled bugs bite two men, one of whom was his own twenty-three-year-old son. Both came down with malaria, but it was a mild form, which they survived.

Once they did become convinced that mosquitoes were the culprit, many concluded the key to conquering malaria was to get rid of the mosquito. No one had any idea how difficult that would be. Unlike smallpox, which lived only in humans and made them very sick, malaria lives in mosquitoes without interfering with their lives much at all. And finding every *Anopheles* mosquito has proved much more difficult than finding all the very sick people with smallpox. Mosquitoes don't read public health posters or turn themselves in for rewards. To conquer plague, we had to learn about the ways of rats and fleas. To fight malaria, we had to learn about mosquitoes.

Few had any concept of the intricate world of the mosquito.

For instance, in Naples, Italy, although fevers raged among its neighbors to the north and south, in Naples itself there were plenty of *Anopheles* but no malaria. It was not enough to understand the parasite, or to understand the disease it caused, to answer this puzzle; scientists also needed to understand the mosquito. So they studied the mosquitoes of Naples and found that although they looked like all the other *Anopheles* the scientists had ever seen, these preferred cow's blood to human blood. A scientist looking into this question convinced a farmer in Naples to move his cows into his dining room. Meanwhile, the scientist and his friend waited in the barn. At nightfall, clouds of *Anopheles* came swarming into the barn, hummed around, and then, finding dinner had moved, headed off toward the dining room. Examination of the blood in these mosquitoes proved the point: it was cow's blood; they bit cattle. Although for years scientists could not tell them apart, it was clear different *Anopheles* species could have very different appetites.

This was only one of the lessons in mosquito habits to be learned in the fight against malaria. Another, learned the hard way, was that mosquitoes have very particular requirements for where they like to breed. When Italy, following America's lead, began to drain its Roman swamps to fight malaria, its malaria rates remained unchanged. European health officials became skeptical. The League of Nations sent a team of experts to the United States in 1927, and decided that there was no reason to listen to American advice. Americans had no malaria compared to Europe, and could therefore know nothing about it. The truth was the Americans could know nothing about the European mosquito. The American *Anopheles* liked warm water; it bred in small pools that had been warmed by the sun, but not in larger bodies of water. The European *Anopheles*, on the other hand, liked cold water just fine. The large ditches built to drain the Italian swamps were a wonderful place for it to breed: draining the swamps benefited these mosquitoes.

Knowing that mosquitoes were the culprit did not make them easy to avoid. Just to convince people to use screens to keep the mosquitoes out and then to stay in at night seems like a simple solution; the surprising thing is how hard this can be to achieve. When in the United States, in the 1920s and '30s, the Public Health Service focused efforts on getting the homes of the poor screened, their instructions spelled out how to cover every single possible hole in the house, and how to do it cheaply: how to build screen doors, how to cover knotholes in wood with flattened tin cans, how to caulk holes in walls and ceilings with papier-mâché. They admonished not to forget the fireplace: the author of one set of instructions claims to have collected as many as 120 *Anopheles* in a room whose only opening was a chimney. Fireplaces were being used year round to heat irons, so they could not merely be closed off: they required their own easily removable but tight-fitting screens to keep the mosquitoes out. Even with all this, the instructions cautioned, not every mosquito will be impeded. Some will sneak in, no matter what, so every home should feature a handy swatter.

As people began to make more money and receive a better education in the southern United States, they could afford to mosquito-proof their homes and they could afford quinine. Mosquito-proofing a small house and keeping the screens in repair for a year cost about $100 in 1944. That would be for only a small house, with about four windows. In some parts of the world, that was more money than a family could make in many years: most families in those areas could not afford screens and quinine. Unfortunately, those were the same parts of the world where malaria flourished. Malaria, like so many diseases, persisted in a belt around the equator where the weather is the hottest and the people the poorest.

Besides keeping mosquitoes out, we could also try to kill them, but that was not so simple either. The problem was to find a poison that worked on mosquitoes but not humans, one that was both cheap and easy to use. When such a chemical was found, it was greeted with great enthusiasm by a world weary of malaria. That chemical was dichloro-diphenyl-trichloro-ethane, better known as DDT. Unlike old insecticides that had to be reapplied weekly, just one gram of DDT per square meter of wall continued to kill *Anopheles* for ten months. If during that time everyone with a fever was treated with quinine, all the malaria parasites in the area would be killed.

In the 1950s the World Health Organization seized upon the discovery of this pesticide as an opportunity to rid the world of malaria. Yet, even in its bold proposal, it admitted some hesitation: Africa, the most malarious continent, presented barriers that seemed as if they might be insurmountable. The climate of much of the continent was ideal for the mosquito, while the dispersed villages scattered across miles of roadless terrain were very difficult to spray. On top of that, many people were illiterate, making it very difficult to spread the word about the campaign. And those were some of the barriers that they could foresee.

There were several problems no one imagined. Sometimes poisoning the mosquitoes had unexpected, disastrous consequences. There was the case of Borneo, for instance. In Borneo, DDT killed the mosquitoes and was also ingested by roaches. The roaches did not die, but they got so much DDT in their systems that when the lizards that live on house walls in the tropics ate the roaches, they became sick. The sick lizards were so slow and uncoordinated that the cats could catch them easily. But the poisoned lizards killed the cats, leaving no cats to chase the rats. The rats began to move boldly into the villages, raising fears of plague. Risk of one disease had been traded for another! New cats had to be airlifted into the villages to drive away the rats.

Other unforeseen obstacles arose. Not long after people began using DDT, it became clear that some mosquitoes had found a way to live with the chemical. Just as drug-resistant tuberculosis could evolve in the human body, so could DDT-resistant *Anopheles* evolve in the wild. As one leader in the fight for eradication was to say, "Nature has dealt us a bitter surprise." At first it seemed that resistance could be outrun. It took five to ten years for resistant mosquitoes to appear, and if DDT was thoroughly sprayed in an area, eliminating all *Anopheles* for a long enough period to eradicate malaria parasites, then perhaps by the time a significant number of mosquitoes were resistant, there would be no more malaria for them to transmit. Unfortunately, the problems of spraying the inside wall of every house in a malarious area so that not a single human-blood-seeking Anopheles mosquito was missed were overwhelming. Humans did not prove to be thorough enough to overcome the mosquitoes' persistence. After hundreds of millions of dollars had been spent, malaria had been eradicated in only ten of the fifty-two nations that had attempted it. Most of the ten successes were easy wins: four were in Europe, five were Caribbean islands, and the tenth was Chile. They had features that made eradication straightforward, such as mild climates, good roads, stable governments, and literate populations. In other places, although the number of cases was greatly reduced, malaria was to rebound. India, for example, had only 50,000 cases in 1961, down from seventy-five million ten years earlier, but by 1965 there were 100,000 cases of the disease, and in 1992 the number of cases was back up to over two million.

India had overcome nearly impossible odds to bring malaria rates so low. Starting in the most affected areas, teams set out to

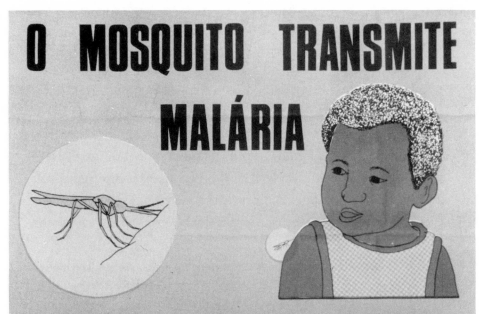

O MOSQUITO TRANSMITE MALÁRIA

EVITE AS PICADAS DO MOSQUITO

ele nasce nas aguas estagnadas,
tape-as perto da casa

coloque redes nas janelas

A malaria control poster from Mozambique urges homeowners to cover stagnant water, where mosquitoes like to breed, and to screen windows

spray the inside walls of each house at least once a year. They had to be sprayed at just the time of year when the mosquitoes were freshly hatched—which varied with the seasonal monsoon rains. And then there were the everyday problems: people were not home when the sprayers came; or they were home, but they wouldn't let them in; or they would let them spray, but not in every room. In one village of sixty-three homes, an inspector found that forty-six were not sprayed for just such reasons. Sometimes heavy rain turned roads into impassable swamps just when the

Doing his part in the great, doomed malaria eradication project launched in the 1950s, a health worker sprays a dwelling in the Yucatán, Mexico

mosquitoes were hatching. Sometimes nomadic people who lived in remote, unsprayed tents part of the year would catch malaria and then bring it back home to their village. The consequence of one infected person in a malaria-free area could be catastrophic: one carrier could remain infective for eighty days, time enough to cause 50,000 new cases of malaria. And if the area had been malaria-free for an extended period of time, eliminating constant reinfection, all the people would have lost their natural immunity: an infection with malaria was much more likely to prove fatal.

Perhaps even more troubling than the ecological consequences of DDT or the problem of resistant mosquitoes was the plight of people in areas where malaria was successfully eliminated for a number of years, only to return. This was the situation in the highlands of Madagascar, an island nation off the coast of Africa, where in the 1950s, when attempts began to eradicate the disease, malaria was the major cause of death. The spraying seemed so successful that by the 1970s Madagascar began to phase out its program. Then, in the 1980s, the malaria returned. As people were no longer immune, the epidemics were deadly: in one three-month period, tens of thousands of people died. This episode left people fearing that trying to eradicate malaria and failing could be worse than not trying at all.

SWEET WORMWOOD

It is a good strategy for a disease to hide part-time in an insect: it becomes a nimble, moving target, able to outdo the Roman Empire, able to withstand a modern-day billion-dollar, world-wide attack. Today, those who battle malaria recommend the use of mosquito nets sprayed with bug killer, and they search for new drugs to kill the drug-resistant parasites.

Some researchers look back to the success of fever-tree bark and ask if there could be another plant holding the key to killing drug-resistant forms of this parasite. They scrutinize the thousands of plants used by healers for fever, searching for one that might kill *Plasmodium*. They have found one plant which gives them great hope. The Chinese medicinal herb qinghao, a plant that we call sweet wormwood, has been used for centuries—it was recommended for use against fevers by a Chinese medical book published in A.D. 341.

In 1971 Chinese scientists first tested the plant, and by 1979 they had shown conclusively that it worked against the most severe types of malaria. Chinese companies have since manufactured the drug, and it is used in China. Even with these hopeful results, however, there are still problems: the drug is not widely available. In today's world, it takes more than a generous cardinal to distribute a drug. It takes more money than the wealth of many generous cardinals combined. One can't just pass out plants as the cardinal once distributed bark. A drug company must manufacture the pure drug, which must then be tested to see that it is safe and effective. This process is both expensive and risky for a drug company to undertake. It could spend millions developing a drug and then find in tests that it is not safe and cannot be sold. A drug like qinghao that has been used for years and seems both safe and effective could be a good gamble. But there is another problem with drugs to treat a disease like malaria: malaria strikes people in the hot parts of the planet, people who are mostly poor. These people have little money to spend on drugs, and they live in a world far away from most drug companies.

It is hard to imagine, when one sits in St. Louis, or Boston, or New Orleans, that less than two hundred years ago the night air could have been deadly. And it is harder still to imagine that the night air could be deadly this very night for almost half of the people in the world. It has been so for as long as we have walked the planet, and it may continue to be so for a long time to come.

CHOLERA

DEATH FROM THE TOWN PUMP

On the morning of June 16, 1832, New Yorkers awoke to the news they had been dreading. All the previous fall and winter, ships streaming into the great port of New York had carried grim stories of a new deadly disease making its way across Europe. The blue cholera, as it was called, overcame people so quickly that they could leave the house for work in the morning pink-cheeked and healthy and be dead by evening. Victims were suddenly struck with horrible cramps, violent vomiting, and diarrhea: their face, hands, and feet shriveled and turned blue-black. Hamburg, London, and Paris—all places less than a two months' sail away—were reeling from the disease. That fall and winter, New York had remained uninfected. The width of the Atlantic Ocean and the quarantine regulations the port saw fit to establish seemed protection enough. But on June 15 a steamship that arrived from the north had brought the grim news: cholera had crossed the Atlantic.

The deadly specter of cholera sneaks up on New York City in this 1883 cartoon while science is asleep on its watch

A passenger aboard the steamship reported that sixty people were dead in Quebec, Canada, of cholera when he left there on Tuesday morning, the twelfth. The worried New Yorkers could only imagine what had happened in the days since. All their news came days late, the time it took to travel by steamship from Quebec to Montreal to New York City via Lake Champlain and the Hudson River. *The Morning Courier* and *New York Enquirer* of June 16, 1832, reported:

A gentleman who left Quebec on Tuesday morning (12th) . . . described the disease as exceeding in malignity any previous accounts of its virulence either in Europe or Asia and all who were attacked were considered hopeless. He witnessed its first symptoms upon five emigrants standing upon the wharf, and before they could be conveyed to the hospital, two of them died. A servant woman living in the house where he boarded was seized with the disease and died within three hours, and a crockery merchant of his acquaintance living in the upper town was carried off within six hours! Three persons were attacked on board the steamboat in which he came passenger to Montreal, and before they reached the next landing, one of them, a resident Canadian, was a corpse—the other two could not have survived.

According to the story, the disease had come to Quebec aboard the *James Carricks*, which had carried 133 Irish immigrants from the port of Dublin. Apprehensive New Yorkers looked out into their own harbor at the vessels coming into port low in the water under their load. Many of the immigrants were coming to New York via Canada, as the fare was cheaper than a direct sailing to New York from Europe.

The mayor of New York called for a quarantine immediately. He ruled that no ship could come within three hundred yards of the city and no vehicle within a mile and a half without being declared cholera-free by the Board of Health. Silently, many New Yorkers asked, what good could a quarantine do? No one knew what caused this horrible disease. Cholera had mysteriously crossed every cordon sanitaire. These lines of soldiers posted to prevent anyone from passing and carrying the disease across Europe had done nothing to stop it. It was clear that, despite quarantines, cholera still broke out in the dirty, crowded port cities. Could it be that there was something about crowded, filthy places themselves that gave rise to the disease? New Yorkers, looking around, were filled with fear as they realized that they could not imagine a more crowded or filthy place.

Crowded city streets piled high with garbage are the perfect place for "King Cholera" to reign in this 1852 British cartoon

New York, a city of nearly a quarter of a million people, had no sewer system, no clean water supply, and no effective garbage collection. Everyone who could afford to had drinking water brought in by cart from country springs; only the poor drank from the city pumps. The only street cleaners were the pigs that roamed the city, feeding on the garbage and filth. Not only did these pigs add to the general excrement in the streets but they were mean and dangerous. Children were maimed and even killed by marauding swine.

Pigs were not the only animals in the streets, which were full of people on horseback and in horse-drawn carts. Where there are horses, there will be manure, so the streets were full of that as well. And as there was no refrigeration, if people wanted milk, they had to have a cow close at hand. To get enough milk for all of New York City required huge herds of dairy cows, crowded into the tiny spaces available for them.

Having all these animals in the city had other consequences. For instance, the City Inspector reported that in the month of May in 1853, 439 dead large animals were removed from the streets, as well as the bodies of 71 dogs, 93 cats, 17 sheep, 4 goats, and 19 hogs. This would pose a problem for any city, but was especially disastrous for one without effective garbage collection. Bodies of dead animals could be collected from the streets and taken to be boiled down into tallow to be used for making candles, but these bone-, offal-, and fat-boiling establishments featured piles of rotting carcasses in their yards and vats of boiling animal parts emitting putrid fumes. This would not be a nice place to live next to, and in fact, the city had originally banned these establishments within the city limits. But as the population grew, regulation was not able to keep pace, and fat-boilers became part of urban life.

The city stank. To any New Yorker with a working nose, the smell was sickening, and some believed the smell itself was literally unhealthy. Cholera revived the old argument between the contagionists and those who thought miasmas caused disease. The contagionists pointed to the progress of cholera around the globe: a ship full of blue-faced, agonized immigrants pulled into port and the next moment people were dropping dead around the city. Those sick people brought something with them, they said, and that something caused disease. But those who argued for miasmas shot back: if cholera is so contagious, if it passes from person to person, why is it that the disease doesn't wipe out the doctors and nurses first? How did it cross the cordon sanitaire if sick people did not? Cholera, they said, did not come on a boat; it emerged from the city's filth and rode into one's nose on the foul-smelling air.

The anti-contagionists also took issue with quarantines. Instead of stopping the disease, they argued, the quarantines only stopped commerce, which led to unemployment. Quarantines produced cities full of out-of-work people, who were starving or took to drinking in their despair, and thus left themselves ever more vulnerable to cholera.

This is what Florence Nightingale, founder of nursing as a profession, a woman with great compassion for the sick, wrote in 1867 about contagion as a theory:

> The disease-germ fetish, and the witchcraft-fetish, are the produce of the same mental condition . . . a desire to group together a number of detached phenomena, so as to make a kind of raft on which weak minds can float . . . when either the witchcraft hypothesis, or the disease-germ hypothesis is made the basis of legislation . . . the matter becomes very serious indeed . . . the (so-called) scientific mind of

England is sinking into a condition of abject superstition ... The germ hypothesis, if logically followed out, must stop all human intercourse whatever, on pain or risk of disease or death.

Florence Nightingale was of course wrong about germs, but well intentioned. It was difficult to think about contagion as strictly a scientific question. When the lives of workers depended upon continuing employment, and quarantines suspended work, it seemed immoral to many to call for quarantines. Instead, it seemed more humane to argue, as the miasma believers did, that, to end the epidemics, cities needed to clean up their streets, regulate housing, and provide clean water. And although they were wrong about germs, miasma believers were right in their methods. Cholera is carried by a germ, not a miasma, but the germ is carried by sewage-contaminated water. With both sides at least somewhat correct, it is no wonder that this argument raged on and on, confusing health advocates, and leaving everyone unsure what to do to escape the disease.

Whether they believed in germs or miasmas, when they heard that cholera had reached Canada, many fearful New Yorkers decided to get out of their stinking city. Those who could afford to headed for their summer country homes, taking along a bottle of laudanum, a sedative incorrectly thought to be effective against cholera. Those who remained frequented the busy Wall Street for news of the epidemic. On Friday, June 29, many remaining New Yorkers fasted and prayed that they might be spared from the devastation of cholera. Only a handful knew that it was already too late.

Three days before the fast day, on Tuesday, June 26, an Irish immigrant by the name of Fitzgerald was struck down with a violent illness. By the time the doctor arrived the next day, Fitzgerald was feeling somewhat better, but two of his children had come

In this mockery of the many ways that Berliners tried to ward off cholera, a gentleman wears protective foot covers, carries both a steaming potion on his head and herbs in his hands to ward off infection, and drags all his household goods behind him so he can leave town in an instant

down with the disease. The children died on Wednesday, and their mother on Friday, as the city prayed and fasted. Although all the doctors who saw them were convinced that the Fitzgeralds had cholera, the Board of Health and the mayor, fearing panic, declined to make a public announcement. Word traveled only by rumor, but travel it did, as did the disease. The roads and rivers leading from New York were soon crowded with people hurrying out of town. By the first week in July some neighborhoods were ghostly silent, with grass beginning to find its way up between the cobblestones. On July 2 the Board of Health finally made its announcement: nine cases of cholera had been confirmed. By the end of the month, it would be reporting a hundred deaths a day.

EVERY CORNER OF THE EARTH

Although unknown outside India before 1817, cholera has made its way, using speedy modern methods of travel, to just about every part of the globe in the past 180 years. Only places very far north, such as Siberia and Iceland, and very far south, such as Antartica, as well as a few isolated islands have been spared. It is a pretty good track record for a germ that cannot survive out of water, cannot survive in sunlight for more than about seven hours, and even in moist shade lives only for a matter of days outside a body. Cholera needs to hitch a ride in a larger organism to travel any distance.

Cholera could have been hiding for thousands of years in India. The Indian peninsula, bordered on two sides by sea and on the third by deserts and mountains, including the highest in the world, the Himalayas, used to be so difficult to reach that its trade goods were rare treasures in the West. Five hundred years ago traders traveling overland across the mountains and vast arid plateaus of Afghanistan and Persia, or those who sailed across the Arabian Sea and up the Persian Gulf and then crossed the Syrian Desert in caravans, were lucky to make the journey in one year. In 1497, when the Portuguese explorer Vasco da Gama sailed around the southern tip of Africa, he opened up a new trade route between Europe and India that was twice as fast. This dangerous journey still took six months, yet it was the fastest route for the next four hundred years. It was not until steamships began to travel between India and the Red Sea in the 1830s that a more rapid route to India opened up. At just about that time, cholera took off to see the world.

In its first pandemic, raging from 1817 to 1823, cholera traveled to some of India's neighbors, Nepal, Ceylon, and Burma, and from there to Southeast Asia, China, Japan, and the Philippines, as well as to Zanzibar and Somalia in Africa. On its second trip out into the world, in the 1830s, when it first visited New York, cholera was to travel to Afghanistan, the Middle East, Russia, and northern Europe before coming to Canada and the United States, and then in the next couple of years to Cuba, Mexico, southern and eastern Europe, and Libya, the Sudan, and Ethiopia. By the end of the nineteenth century, cholera reached South America and spread along the whole east coast of Africa.

The Masai tribe of the East African highlands was to fall to cholera in the nineteenth century. At the time, the Masai dominated a huge area in what is now the country of Kenya. Their livelihood was cattle and they waged warfare to collect more cattle. In 1865 cholera struck at Mecca, in Arabia, among the Muslim pilgrims gathered for the annual pilgrimage. As pilgrims returned to their homes across Asia, Africa, and Europe, they carried the disease with them. Cholera crossed the Red Sea into Ethiopia, and trading caravans carried it inland. When Masai warriors returned from raiding the Soma-Gurra, a tribe to their north that was especially rich in camels, horses, and cattle, they brought cholera back with them. The disease raged through Masailand. This devastating epidemic, followed by smallpox a few years later, marked the end of the reign of the Masai over the region. Caravans trading beads and cotton for ivory and slaves were to carry the epidemic all the way south to the island of Zanzibar, where it killed 20,000 people in four months.

In the United States, even the wild and remote West was not free from cholera. From St. Louis west, until you reached the budding coastal towns of California, the country was sparsely populated by Native Americans and small groups of pioneers. This vast stretch of land was known as the "Great American Desert." But into this wilderness, in the spring of 1849, set out a string of intrepid pioneers. Word of gold in California brought eighty thousand gold seekers in 1849. Just before they streamed west, taking sailing ships around South America, or steamships to Panama, or setting out overland and braving the desert, the third pandemic of cholera had reached the East Coast.

The more than forty thousand gold seekers who chose the overland route brought with them sixty thousand oxen, mules, and horses. They traveled by stagecoach and railroad as far west as Missouri and then camped, waiting for the spring to mature the prairie grasses to feed their stock on the trip farther west. The camps grew crowded with eager "forty-niners." They slept in tents or just on the ground and tramped into mud the banks of the rivers where they drew their water and took their baths. Cholera broke out among them.

When they did set out into the great wilderness, the forty-niners carried the disease with them. Major Osborne Cross, who led a group of military men over the Oregon Trail in 1849, wrote in his journal:

> *May 26, 1849*
>
> *It would be useless to attempt to enumerate the deaths that occurred among the emigrants. The graves along the road too plainly told us that the cholera was prevailing to an alarming extent. At this point we were one hundred and thirty-eight miles from Fort Leavenworth [Kansas] and one hundred and seventy-two miles from Fort Kearny [Nebraska], entirely cut off from all assistance or the least possible means of getting any relief. It was out of the question to lie by, for, being in the area, we were compelled to move rapidly on to over take the command. It was a serious subject to think of, and I know of no danger that I would not sooner be exposed to than again suffer the uneasiness of mind which I experienced at this time; for we had not*

only full proof of the prevalence of this dreadful scourge along the
road, but were actually carrying it with us in our wagons . . . When
we arose in the morning it was a question among us as to who might
fall a victim to it before another sun.

The gold seekers also brought cholera to the other inhabitants of this vast wilderness: the Native Americans who caught the disease were devastated. Forty-niners recorded how they came across one group of Cherokee camped near the fork of the Platte River, in Nebraska Territory. Out of fourteen, six were dead, one dying, and the rest too ill to bury the others. Even inhabiting this remote place could not protect these Cherokee from the encroachments of the globe-trotting disease. When cholera stole a life, as one forty-niner put it, "It was sometimes just a case of Death snapping his finger at you and you are gone."

THE DESPERATE IMMIGRANT

Cholera was to return to New York four times in the nineteenth century, and in that time the city grew from a town of about 33,000 in 1790 to a bursting-at-the-seams city of 3,437,000 in 1900. People poured into New York from all over Europe. Most of those who would die were the poor and the immigrants; four out of ten were Irish.

Many Irish immigrants were fleeing extreme poverty and famine in their homeland. They were so desperate to leave, and so poor, that they were willing to travel in extremely crowded ships, spending as many as sixty days in the hull of a clipper, sleeping on bunks three deep in the six-foot-high steerage, subsisting on little but oatmeal and water, with their only toilet facilities a slop bucket. They arrived in the city penniless and ragged from their passage.

In the city, the only quarters they could afford were crowded tenements where staying clean was a Herculean task. How crowded? In 1864 the New York City Inspector reported that 900 people were living in two tenement buildings that were each 18 feet wide, 180 feet deep, and five stories high. They shared a privy in the yard, and a pump a block away was their only source of water. All the water for drinking, cooking, and cleaning had to be hauled bucket by bucket down the block and up flights of stairs.

One sixteen-year-old Irish girl who immigrated not to New York but to Quebec, Canada, described how it felt to leave one's home and brave a horrible passage for the dream of a better life and then to arrive in the midst of a cholera epidemic.

Imagine our feelings at finding ourselves in a plague-stricken city where men, women, and children smitten by cholera dropped in the streets to die in agony; where business was paralyzed, and naught prevailed but sorrow mingled with dread and gloom.

And she soon found herself one of those dropping in the streets. As she walked through Quebec City, searching for some kind of work, she was overcome and collapsed, and was swept off to a fever hospital. There she lay on a cot in a ward crowded with hundreds of patients. It was "a veritable house of torture," she wrote, "where the most appalling shrieks, groans, and prayers and curses filled the air continually and, as if in answer to all this, day and night from the shed outside came the tap, tap, tap of the workmen's hammers, as they drove the nails into rough coffins which could not be put together hastily enough for the many whose shrieks subsided into moans, which gradually died away into that silence not to be broken." Although she survived, her three brothers succumbed to the disease. These poor, tattered newcomers were eyed with suspicion by other city dwellers. Did the Irish immigrants' strange habits bring on this disease? Was it their poverty, or their religion? Or was it something that came with the ships full of goods from across the world?

Likewise, immigrants grew suspicious of city officials, who stopped their ships just when they neared their destination, and forced them to stay trapped for days in the dark steerage, sometimes while cholera raged around them, turning the ship into a death trap. The city officials set up roadblocks to prevent them from escaping the cholera-racked city, and established the quarantine that was starving them. The immigrants did not think the officials had their best interests at heart.

As cholera killed the poor all around the world, similar antagonisms between the well-to-do and the less fortunate arose in city after city. In St. Petersburg, Russia, as health officials took to the streets to collect the ill and convey them to hospitals, the poor began to believe the reason they were the only ones dying was because they were being poisoned by the physicians. Riots broke out in which a mob overran the cholera hospital, beat the workers, and liberated the sick.

In Tuscany, Italy, as rumors spread that physicians were poisoning people, doctors found anonymous notes left on their houses threatening to have them torn to pieces and thrown to the dogs.

In New York, officials began removing the bodies of the dead sometimes before relatives had finished their funeral rites. In one case, a whole tenement building banded together to block officials from removing a body by the stairway. The officials finally lowered the coffin out of the window to the ground.

On the night of June 14, 1832, two weeks before the Irish immigrant Fitzgerald became ill with New York City's first recorded case of cholera, the city marshal of Albany, New York—

aware of the outbreak in Canada—stopped three immigrant-laden boats at a lock a mile north of the city for inspection. The crew and passengers began to protest violently. The immigrants feared the authorities would not let them pass and would perhaps force their return to cholera-ridden Montreal. An attempt was made to force open the lock. The marshal responded by removing the cranks from the mechanism, immobilizing it, thereby confirming the passengers' worst fears. In the hubbub and the darkness, the marshal hardly noticed the dark figures that began leaping from the boats to the nearby bank. When he finally did see them, he could do nothing to prevent the immigrants, who had braved terrible hardships to get this far, from fleeing into the darkness and making their way to the city by foot.

Word got out on the immigrant grapevine the very next day that canal boats approaching Albany from the north were being stopped and immigrants were being held at the locks. Hearing this, immigrants coming down from the north transferred above Albany to boats coming from the west, and thus passed on down to all points south, including New York City, without inspection.

A PUMP HANDLE

Into all this confusion and death entered one man who was not only to find an answer to the mysteries of cholera but also to teach the world a whole new way to explore what causes a disease. That man was John Snow, who became a pioneer epidemiologist, or expert in the study of epidemics. Unlike bacteriologists such as Pasteur, Koch, and their followers, Snow would not concentrate on looking for how a particular bug caused illness in a particular individual. Instead, he would try to trace the trail that the germ left through a population. His tool would be not the microscope but rather the survey. He would look at the people who got the disease and those who did not, and try to figure out how one group differed from the other. This would lead him to understand how the disease was transmitted.

John Snow was born in York, England, on June 15, 1813, the eldest son of a farmer. He was an independent thinker from the beginning. At seventeen he decided to become a vegetarian, and about that time he also gave up all intoxicating drink. Later he helped introduce the use of ether to put people to sleep during surgery. In the 1850s he began to study cholera. He noted that people who had cholera had digestive troubles immediately. From what he had seen he reflected that if a disease was caused by something that was inhaled or injected, a person would have other symptoms before a stomachache. Cholera, he suggested, was probably caused by something taken directly into the digestive system, by something that people ate or drank. Snow then theorized that if cholera invaded the intestinal system, and was present in the vomit and diarrhea so violently discharged from its victims, all it would take to spread the disease would be for a tiny bit of this material to somehow get into the food or drink of someone else. He pointed out that among the poor in the cities, where water was so hard to come by, it would be very difficult to have enough water to wash thoroughly, and contamination would be very easy.

Snow went on to reason that if this was the only way for the disease to spread, then it would not spread beyond the very poor; however, if it was possible for the water that people drank from rivers and from pumps throughout the town to become contaminated, then the disease could spread far and wide.

Then Snow took one more brilliant step: he set out to test his theory. First, he examined in minute detail the circumstances of one single cholera outbreak in London, one he called "the most

terrible outbreak of cholera which ever occurred in this kingdom." "Within two hundred and fifty yards of the spot where
Cambridge Street joins Broad Street," he wrote, "there were
upwards of five hundred attacks of cholera in ten days . . . the
mortality would no doubt have been greater if it were not for
the flight of the population." Snow immediately suspected that
the pump used by most people in the neighborhood, which stood
very close to this intersection, was the source of the contagion.
When he looked at the water from the pump, however, it
appeared clear and clean. But Snow wondered if it were possible
for the water still to be impure even though it appeared fresh, and
he pondered how to examine his theory. At this time, no one had
yet found a germ that caused a disease. It was 1854: it would be
nineteen years before Hansen saw the little sticks that would come
to be known as *Mycobacterium leprae* under his microscope.

Snow went to London's General Register Office and asked for
the names and addresses of all the people who had died from
cholera in the first three days of the epidemic. There were eighty-
three. Then he went back to the neighborhood and found that all
these people had lived near the Broad Street pump. Out of eighty-
three, only ten lived close to a different pump. Of these ten, five
had preferred to drink from the Broad Street pump even though
it was farther away, and three were children who had gone to
school near the Broad Street pump, two of whom were known to
drink the water. Only two out of the eighty-three who died of the
disease were not known to drink from the Broad Street pump.
John Snow took his results to the neighborhood council, and the
very next day they removed the handle of the pump so that no
one else could use it.

Although convinced that he was on the right track, Snow did
not consider these pump stories to be irrefutable proof of the
cause of the disease. There could be something else that all these

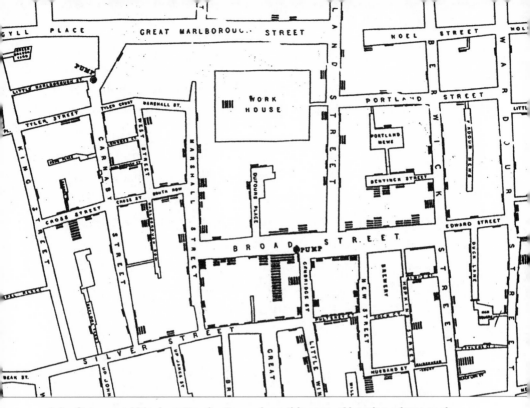

John Snow used black rectangles to mark on this map of London where each person who had cholera lived. Note concentration around the Broad Street pump

people had in common, as unlikely as that seemed, which could be the true cause for their disease. For instance, they could have all bought bread from the same infected bakery.

Then Snow realized an opportunity for an even better test of his theory. Two competing water companies supplied piped-in water to homes in London: they were the Lambeth Company and the Southwark and Vauxhall Company. Their customers were so intermixed that next-door neighbors often had different water companies. One company, the Lambeth, took in water from the Thames River upstream from where the London sewage entered the water. The other company, Southwark and Vauxhall, took in water downstream from this point. Therefore, the Lambeth water could not be tainted by sewage, whereas the water delivered by the Southwark and Vauxhall Company could. This was a great opportunity to see if sewage-contaminated water caused cholera. Snow obtained a list of cholera deaths from the city and then set out to determine which houses used water from each company. This was not an easy task: Snow had to go door-to-door asking each family. Many were renters who never paid the water bill and therefore had no idea which company they used. Not to be forestalled, Snow examined the water from the two companies and developed a simple chemical test to tell their water apart.

After Snow himself found that out of forty-four dead, thirty-eight used water from the Southwark and Vauxhall Company, city officials took over the investigation. These are their findings:

Water Source	Number of Houses	Deaths from Cholera	Deaths per 10,000 Houses
Southwark & Vauxhall	40,046	1,263	315
Lambeth	26,107	98	37
Other	256,423	1,422	59

John Snow wrote of this survey:

The experiment was on the grandest scale. No fewer than three hundred thousand people of both sexes, of every age and occupation, and of every rank and station, from gentlefolks down to the very poor, were divided into two groups without their choice and, in most cases, without their knowledge; one group being supplied with water containing the sewage of London, and, amongst it, whatever might have come from the cholera patients, the other group having water quite free from such impurity.

One could hardly ask for more conclusive results: while in 10,000 houses supplied by the Lambeth Company, only 37 deaths occurred, in 10,000 supplied by the Southwark and Vauxhall, there were 315. It certainly appeared that the sewage-tainted water had carried cholera into these homes.

A DARING DRINK

It would seem that Snow's demonstration would be convincing: Londoners had not been divided by their ethnicity, nor was it the poor who got sick and the rich who stayed well. But, despite Snow's apparent triumph, not everyone was convinced cholera was caused by waterborne contagion. There still remained the problem of finding the actual cause of these cholera infections. Even after 1883, when Robert Koch was to discover in more than

Before John Snow, sewage in the water was suspected but not proven to be unhealthful. In 1828 cartoonist George Cruikshank depicted the owner of the Southwark waterworks, John Edwards, sitting on the waterworks intake point. In his caption, Cruikshank called Edwards "Lord of the Man-ure of Shetland" and "Agitator-in-Chief of the Intestinal Canals"

one hundred victims of the fifth cholera pandemic a tiny, comma-shaped creature that appeared to cause the disease, some people remained skeptical. Like Florence Nightingale, people feared that to agree that cholera was contagious might mean massive quarantines and no work for the poor. Also, a growing number of people had become devoted to making cities clean, healthy places. These "sanitarians" had a vision of how to transform cities from filthy, crowded places to beautiful places to live. Frederick Law Olmsted, a designer of New York City's Central Park and parks in many other cities, was one such thinker. Of cities, Olmsted wrote: "Our country has entered upon a stage of progress in which its welfare is to depend on the convenience, safety, order and economy of life in its great cities. It cannot gain in virtue, wisdom, comfort, except as they also advance."

After Koch's discovery of the actual microbe that caused cholera in 1883, some sanitarians argued even more fervently that cholera was due to filth. Some feared that if people thought a germ, and not miasma, caused the disease, they would abandon sanitation and leave cities swimming in muck. Even if they did not dispute that the germ Koch discovered caused the disease, they were certain that the germ alone was not sufficient.

The most outspoken of these critics was Max von Pettenkofer. We probably would not know his name if his father had been wealthy. But Max's father could not afford to provide for all his eight children, and so Max was raised by his uncle, a chemist, from the age of nine. The boy went on to study chemistry and medicine and to work tirelessly and with great passion. He was very successful: in his lifetime, methods he developed were used to restore oil paintings; to assess the amount of silver or gold in a hunk of ore; to reproduce an ancient form of red glass (winning Max the favor of the kings of Bavaria); and to tell if a person had been poisoned by arsenic.

Pettenkofer became devoted as well to improving the quality of life in cities, which motivated him to prove that the cholera germ alone did not cause cholera. Like Olmsted, Pettenkofer thought cities should have parks just for the sake of their beauty. He also called upon cities to educate people about cleanliness and good nutrition, and to provide clean water and sanitation. Well-fed people living in well-ventilated, uncrowded homes, with fresh running water piped in for convenient washing, would not get cholera, he argued. And about this, Pettenkofer *was* right, but not for his reasons. Clean water, water not contaminated with sewage, would not carry the cholera germ into people's homes.

To prove the germ did not cause the disease, Max von Pettenkofer resolved to perform on himself what he called the crucial experiment: he decided to swallow the microbe that causes cholera. On October 7, 1892, when Pettenkofer was seventy-four years of age, he received a fresh culture of the bacillus taken from the stool of a patient dying of cholera in Hamburg. Pettenkofer mixed the culture into a little bouillon, poured himself a small measure, and drank it, on an empty stomach. He made sure to point out that the number of the bacilli he was swallowing in his cocktail was far more than the number one would normally ingest in an accidental exposure. What happened? The lucky man experienced no symptoms other than light diarrhea that proved to contain a great number of the bacilli. Pettenkofer said of his risky experiment:

I have the right to regard myself as a "vile body." I am seventy-four years old . . . I have not a single tooth left and use my false teeth only when I have to speak distinctly and at length, not while I am eating; and I also feel the other burdens of old age. Even if I were deceiving myself and the experiment put my life at risk, I would look death calmly in the eye, for it would be no irresponsible or cowardly suicide

that I underwent, I would be dying in the service of science, like a sol-
dier on the field of honor. Health and life are, as I have so often said,
very great earthly goods, but not the highest for man. Man, if he will
rise above the animals, must sacrifice both life and health for the
higher ideals.

Believing as we do today that the bacillus alone causes cholera, we find it hard to explain why Max von Pettenkofer survived his deadly drink. The best explanation may be good luck. It is also true that although a drink of cholera should give any person the disease, Pettenkofer was right in his approach to prevention. Cleaning up the city, not isolating the bacillus, is the essential step to eliminating cholera. Even though the discovery of the bacillus led to the creation of a vaccine and the use of antibiotics in treatment, the key to preventing and curing cholera is providing clean water, that is—although Pettenkofer refused to acknowledge it—water that is not contaminated with the cholera bacillus.

CHOLERA TODAY

Although it emerged out of the distant past, cholera continues to find the modern world a hospitable place. In 1970, a cholera outbreak in West Africa caused an estimated 150,000 cases and 20,000 deaths. The disease traveled first in contaminated water along the coast, probably spread by fishermen. Then it quickly swung inland; as people ran from the devastation, they carried the disease with them. Festivals, fairs, and celebrations often turned into deadly outbreaks of cholera: at one feast where ten thousand gathered to celebrate the circumcision of a sultan's son, thousands of cases and hundreds of deaths occurred.

The tragedy of these deaths is that they occurred at a time when we know what causes cholera and how to treat it. The wrinkled hands and blue face of the victims occur because they have lost so

Rwandan refugees in 1994 draw from their only source of water, Lake Kivu, despite the fact that the lake is contaminated both by human waste from their crowded camps and by the bodies of the dead

much fluid in their vomit and diarrhea. The germ that causes cholera releases a toxin that jams tiny pumps in the lining of our intestines, causing them to draw water out of the body. Stomach acid kills the cholera germ, so one must swallow a lot of bacilli for any to survive to reach the intestine. Those that do, however, are comfortable in the intestine, and there lock on the pumps, causing the volumes of watery diarrhea that can leave sufferers so extremely dehydrated that their blood thickens and can no longer flow. Such severe dehydration can be fatal. To prevent death, all cholera patients need is water, lots and lots of clean water, and a little sugar and salt, to replace all the fluid they are losing. Over the course of four days, patients could need as much as their bodies' weight in water. But they really need nothing other than this. The infection will end on its own if victims can just live through the dehydration.

When cholera broke out in Peru in 1991, launching the first cholera epidemic in South America in this century, health officials were able to treat people effectively, and instead of half of the infected people dying, the disease killed as few as 1 out of 100 of those infected.

Even though we know how to treat it and how to avoid it, cholera continues to thrive where there are crowds of people without proper sanitation. When war refugees poured out of the African country of Rwanda in 1994, cholera broke out in their crowded camps. In the disorder following the breakup of the Soviet Union, disease has plagued the former Soviet republics: in the summer of 1994, 2,000 people were hospitalized for cholera, and 34 died. During the summer of 1995 cholera was found in the river in Moscow. Where people are not getting the simple, most basic things they need to stay healthy—a clean place to live and pure water—cholera will follow. And as Max von Pettenkofer foresaw, the key to preventing this disease is not cures but cleaning up.

AIDS

A PLAGUE IS BORN

When Marcus Conant was growing up in Florida, his father played a game with him. He gave his son a penny and asked which he would rather have, a million dollars or the penny doubled every day for a month. Marcus, of course, went for the million dollars. Then his father sat him down and with paper and pen calculated his folly. A penny doubled every day for a month amounted to more than five million dollars.

When he was a forty-four-year-old dermatologist in San Francisco, Conant would put his doubling lesson to good use. In April 1981 his friend Dr. Alvin Friedman-Kien called to tell him of a few cases of a rare cancer in young gay men. Kaposi's sarcoma, or KS, as it would come to be known, was so rare in the United States that most doctors had seen it only in textbooks. In its rare occurrences here, usually in old men, the disease caused purple spots or lesions to appear on the skin, and sometimes on the internal organs, and gradually, over decades, might prove fatal. But

Since 1987 more than 42,000 three-by-six-foot quilted panels have been made in memory of people who have died of AIDS, forming a memorial quilt that covers twenty-seven acres

Friedman-Kien told of young gay men with KS who had ravaging cases of this disease, with the purple blotches forming quickly on their skin, inside their mouths, in their throats, and on their internal organs. Conant lived and worked in a San Francisco neighborhood known as the Castro, a center of gay life in the nation. If this disease was now attacking young homosexual men, it would certainly be finding its way to his neighborhood. The next day, as Conant was speaking to dermatologists at the University of San Francisco, he asked if anyone had seen any strangely virulent KS. A hand went up: one doctor had a patient in the hospital with the disease at that very moment. He was a young gay man named Kenneth Horne.

Conant went to the university and asked for space to start a clinic where doctors could send their patients with this disease. He would volunteer his time to see the patients. Conant, once fooled by the pennies, paid attention not to how few cases doctors were seeing but to how rapidly the number of cases found seemed to be increasing. He felt certain there would be many more. The cases he had heard about had gone for months before they were diagnosed. At that moment there might be other patients sitting in dermatologists' offices with these strange purple lesions, being told by doctors, correctly, that they resembled nothing known to be serious, and not to worry. Conant became determined to spread the word that there was a new form of Kaposi's sarcoma out there, and to find what was causing it. When the clinic opened on September 21, 1981, staffed by Conant, cancer doctor Paul Volberding, and several others, no one knew that they had begun what was to be the first AIDS clinic in the world.

A trail of startlingly similar young men trickled in to the Kaposi's clinic. They were in their thirties, gay, and along with KS they had an array of other strange conditions. They suffered from endless diarrhea, night sweats, and white patches of yeast growing in their mouths. Some had contracted a pneumonia caused by *Pneumocystis carinii.* This common fungus infects nearly everyone but causes disease only in those whose immune systems are very disabled. These young men's lymph nodes—the filters of the body's drainage system, where their immune cells would be alerted to invaders—were swollen and hard as if a terrible infection was occurring. And blood tests found that the levels of certain disease-fighting immune cells were very low. Another thing these men had in common was that they tended to be very sexually active, often having several sexual partners in one night several times a week.

Conant and the others drew careful maps of the men's Kaposi's sarcoma and peered down their throats to look for its purple lesions. They ran their fingers along their necks, armpits, and groins, looking for hard, swollen lymph nodes. They drew their blood and collected their urine, and took small pieces of their lesions to study.

The doctors themselves were young men, some of them were gay. Looking at the patients' bodies was almost like looking in the mirror, except it was the mirror of their nightmares, where their skin was covered by growing purple lesions. They didn't know what caused their patients' strange afflictions, but they became more and more convinced that they were seeing an epidemic caused by a germ that found some way to get from body to body. Now they were touching these men's skin and looking down their throats and examining their blood and urine. Conant began to measure the levels of immune cells in his own blood on a regular basis.

On November 30, 1981, Kenneth Horne died. His was the first case of Kaposi's sarcoma in San Francisco that Conant had learned of, and his was to be the first case of the disease that would come to be known as AIDS reported to the government agency that tracks epidemics, the Centers for Disease Control (CDC). This young man, who had walked into a doctor's office complaining of tiredness, diarrhea, and two purple spots, one on his leg and one near his nipple, died one year later blind and skeletally thin, suffocated by a pneumonia his immuno-compromised body could not fight off. When his doctors examined his body at autopsy, they found the KS had spread to his lungs, spleen, bladder, and adrenal glands. In addition, his eyes were infected by a virus known as CMV, and two fungi—*Crypto-coccus,* which is commonly found in bird droppings, and *Pneu-mocystis carinii.*

A VIRUS FOR OUR TIMES

The virus that caused this frightening new disease was well suited to start an epidemic that would be hard to find and hard to stop. As with leprosy and tuberculosis, it was usually years from the time one was infected with the virus until one first showed symptoms of disease. But all the while, when one was silently infected, one could be passing the virus to others unwittingly. When the disease did surface, it came in a variety of disguises. Because the virus that causes AIDS, *h*uman *i*mmunodeficiency *v*irus, or HIV, damages the immune system of the people it infects, they catch all sorts of other diseases that their immune system would normally ward off. So AIDS (*A*cquired *I*mmuno*d*eficiency *S*yndrome) appears in the form of a variety of other afflictions, such as Kaposi's sarcoma and *Pneumocystis carinii* pneumonia (PCP). And the ways the virus mainly spreads, through sex and illegal intravenous drug use, are things that people do privately. When John Snow came to the door investigating cholera, people gladly told him which water pump they drank from, but people do not freely reveal their sexual contacts or their drug use.

Yet doctors and scientists, in a startlingly short time, saw

CENTERS FOR DISEASE CONTROL

July 3, 1981 / Vol. 30 / No. 25

Epidemiologic Notes and Reports
305 Kaposi's Sarcoma and *Pneumocystis*
Pneumonia Among Homosexual Men —
New York City and California
308 Cutaneous Larva Migrans in American
Tourists — Martinique and Mexico
314 Measles — U.S. Military

MORBIDITY AND MORTALITY WEEKLY REPORT

Epidemiologic Notes and Reports

Kaposi's Sarcoma and *Pneumocystis* Pneumonia
Among Homosexual Men — New York City and California

During the past 30 months, Kaposi's sarcoma (KS), an uncommonly reported malignancy in the United States, has been diagnosed in 26 homosexual men (20 in New York City [NYC], 6 in California). The 26 patients range in age from 26-51 years (mean 39 years). Eight of these patients died (7 in NYC, 1 in California)—all 8 within 24 months after KS was diagnosed. The diagnoses in all 26 cases were based on histopathological examination of skin lesions, lymph nodes, or tumor in other organs. Twenty-five of the 26 patients were white, 1 was black. Presenting complaints from 20 of these patients are shown in Table 1.

This Centers for Disease Control publication, which reports on disease trends, first mentioned Kaposi's sarcoma in young homosexual men in this article from July 1981. The previous month, five cases of *Pneumocystis carinii* pneumonia in young gay men had been reported

through all these mysteries of the AIDS epidemic. They quickly comprehended that the people who were getting the disease were all related to one another in ways that would allow a virus to pass from one person to the other through their blood or their bodily fluids. As case reports of KS and *Pneumocystis* in previously healthy people came in from New York, San Francisco, and Los Angeles, the Centers for Disease Control began to investigate. In 1981 two CDC epidemiologists began going door-to-door, like John Snow, talking to sufferers from the disease, looking for something that could link them one to the other and reveal what had given them this disease. Between the two of them, Mary Guinan and Harold Jaffe were to interview 75 percent of the patients in the United States at that time. They sought out patients in their hospital rooms and homes and asked them everything they could think of asking: Did anyone in your family have cancer? Tell me about your diet. Have you traveled recently? Were you a soldier in Vietnam? (Maybe the disease was a side effect of exposure to a chemical weapon.) Do you have any pets?

Mary Guinan realized something as she asked these questions: the groups of people infected were the same as those infected by another disease, known as hepatitis B. This disease can be sexually transmitted and can also spread between intravenous drug users who share used needles. Because the disease can be transmitted only by infected bodily fluids, it does not spread between people who live together or work together but only between people who have unprotected sex or share needles. And there was one other way to spread hepatitis B that had not yet shown up in this new epidemic: if this disease truly was contagious in the same way as hepatitis B, it would have gotten into the blood supply, and people who received blood products from blood banks could be infected. Hemophiliacs, who suffer from a bleeding disorder and need regular injections of blood products, would be most at risk. Guinan decided to keep an eye out to see if any hemophiliacs developed this mysterious disease. In June of 1982 the CDC received an order for the drug to treat PCP. The patient, the order read, was a hemophiliac.

By 1983, a mere two years after the report of Kenneth Horne's case, HIV was to be discovered. Together, an American scientist, Robert Gallo, working at the National Cancer Institute, and a French scientist named Luc Montaignier, working at the Pasteur Institute, where the plague-hunter Alexandre Yersin began his career nearly one hundred years before, identified the virus. In the years to come researchers would find that the virus approaches certain cells in the immune system, known as T cells, in such a way that the cells open up and take the virus right inside. Once inside a cell, the virus worms its way into the cell's command center. The virus tells the cell its new job is to make virus. The immune cell is transformed into a virus factory pumping out thousands of viral particles. The cell dies in the process, and its viral progeny go on to infect thousands of other cells.

Early in the infection, as fast as HIV kills an infected T cell, the immune system replaces it with another one. It is a tremendous battle: as many as one billion new virus particles are produced per day. This fight can go on for years, until, finally, the immune system seems to be exhausted. New T cells can no longer be made fast enough, and their numbers begin to drop. With fewer and fewer T cells, the infected person can no longer fend off invaders and begins to succumb to a variety of infections.

WHAT STOPPED US

Marcus Conant felt lucky that the American Academy of Dermatology would hold its annual meeting in San Francisco in December of 1981. The meeting would bring to the city dermatologists from all around the country and give him the perfect opportunity to let them know about this new disease. Conant had a brochure printed up with descriptions of the disease, color photographs of the lesions, and the heading "Disseminated Kaposi's Sarcoma in Young Homosexual Men." There were more than eighty known patients with this disease, the brochure went on to explain, and 17 percent of them had died. And then it informed doctors whom to contact for advice if a patient came in with such a lesion. The volunteers handing out the brochures were shocked by doctors' reactions to it. Most barely glanced at the material. One said, "Homosexuals? We don't have homosexuals where I come from."

Even though twentieth-century science could quickly identify the virus, medicine had no tools to fight prejudice. In the United States, AIDS first appeared in groups of people that others often felt free to hate. For years, much of mainstream America had condemned homosexuality as immoral, causing most gay men and lesbians to keep their sexual preferences secret. But during the decade before this new epidemic, gay men and lesbians had begun to ask that their sexuality be accepted by society, that they could live openly as homosexuals and not face discrimination. One of their first triumphs was to convince the American Psychiatric Association to stop calling homosexuality a mental illness. But this was also a sign of how far they had to go. People known to be homosexuals lost their jobs, were denied places to live, were even beaten up on the street, all because of some people's fierce prejudices against them.

These prejudices led people to ignore the growing epidemic. The news media seemed to take a hands-off approach. Not wanting to talk about homosexuals for fear of offending the public, reporters said nothing at all and failed to alert people early on to the disease in their midst. Ironically, in one of the first network television news stories to cover the disease, in August 1982, anchorman Dan Rather said, "Federal health officials consider it an epidemic. Yet you rarely hear a thing about it." Of course, if anyone was to hear anything about it, it would have to be from people like Dan Rather himself.

Worst of all, government agencies responsible for studying health problems held back funding from AIDS research. Once the virus had been discovered, no one knew how to attack it. Because a virus uses our cells' machinery to reproduce, it is difficult to find a drug that stops viral reproduction without poisoning our own cells in the process. We had no treatment for HIV, and the virus appeared to be killing everyone it infected. At the end of 1983 Congress issued a report criticizing the federal government's lack of response to the AIDS epidemic, saying that "tragically, funding levels for AIDS investigations have been dictated by political considerations rather than by the professional judgment of scientists."

IGNORANCE = FEAR

SILENCE = DEATH   FIGHT AIDS ACT UP

Keith Haring, an artist who died of AIDS, designed this print to encourage people to learn about the disease and spread the word in order to fight the epidemic

Many members of the gay community wanted to ignore the epidemic as well. Not only did gay men fear that news of a disease attacking them, especially a disease that was not only deadly but sexually transmitted, could easily turn even open-minded people against them, but the gay rights movement was based upon the idea that gay sex was not morally wrong. The movement arose in the midst of a broader sexual revolution in which people were rebelling against all sorts of sexual taboos. As gay sex had once been condemned, in the blossoming gay culture the one thing that was now taboo was to tell someone he should not have sex. Some gay communities featured bathhouses where men could go to have sex. At a bathhouse, strangers who found each other agreeable would have sex, and then feel free to move on to other partners if they so desired. It so happened that anonymous sex, between people who hardly knew one another, with many different partners in one night, without the protection of latex condoms, provided the perfect way for a virus to spread.

On April 4, 1984, a gay newspaper in San Francisco published an editorial entitled "Killing the Movement" that included a "traitors list" of gay leaders who were traitors because they supported the idea of closing the bathhouses. In the midst of an epidemic, some saw bathhouses as a disaster and insisted that they be closed to reduce the spread of the disease. But others saw the bathhouses as a shrine to the idea that no expression of sexuality was taboo. Closing the bathhouses was a way of saying gay sex was dirty and wrong, they insisted; it was a step back in their liberation. The newspaper declared that all those gay leaders who supported bathhouse closure were traitors. One of the traitors was Marcus Conant.

Everywhere the virus went, reluctance to attack it seemed to follow. The managers of the nation's blood supply also stood in the way of preventing the spread of the virus in blood products. From the time CDC epidemiologists saw that the disease followed the pattern of hepatitis B, it was suspected that someone treated with blood donated by an infected donor could become infected with the virus. Although the first case of AIDS associated with blood products surfaced in 1982, blood banks failed to take every possible measure to protect the blood supply until 1985. Hemophiliacs, who receive concentrated blood products derived from many donors, were most vulnerable. It is estimated that more than two thirds of hemophiliacs became infected with HIV.

The disease was also transmitted between those who injected illegal intravenous drugs such as heroin when they shared the same needles or syringes. When health workers in New York City attempted to hand out clean needles to addicts to encourage them not to share, and therefore prevent the spread of the disease, the neighborhoods where the needle exchanges were stationed, which were largely minority communities, reacted with anger to the idea. They felt they were being marked as harboring this deadly disease and feared increasing prejudice would follow.

There was ample evidence that people associated with this disease were being persecuted. The disease struck hard in Haiti, perhaps because it was a popular vacation spot for gay Americans. In the early eighties, immigrant Haitian families in New York City were evicted from their homes and Haitian children were beaten up. A letter circulated in south Florida asking employers to fire any Haitians they were employing.

In another town in Florida, in 1986, three young brothers who were all hemophiliacs and infected with HIV were banned from grade school by fearful school authorities and parents. Even though the American Red Cross, the American Medical Association, and the CDC all stated that there was no reason that HIV-infected children should not attend school with everyone else, people remained frightened. A federal court finally overruled the local order and said that the boys could return to school. And they did, for all of one week, before someone burned the family's house to the ground.

In 1990 a senator proposed a bill in Congress to prevent people infected with HIV from working as food handlers. Although scientists said there was no evidence that infected workers were any risk to diners, the senator argued for allowing fear alone to shape legislation: "Call it hysteria or whatever you want, but the vast majority of people who eat in restaurants don't want their food prepared or handled by someone who has AIDS or HIV." Another senator argued against him, saying, "Let science govern. Do what is right . . . Should a homosexual be discriminated against? The answer is no." In the end, thirty-nine senators voted for the legislation, but sixty-one voted against, and it was not passed.

Even fourteen years into the epidemic, in 1995, when a delegation of gay political leaders was invited to the White House, Secret

Service guards put on rubber gloves to inspect the invitees' bags. The guards made two false assumptions: the first was that just because these people were gay they were infected with HIV, and the second was that touching an infected person's belongings could cause infection with the disease. Twelve years after the virus was discovered, nine years after the Surgeon General's report stated that HIV cannot be spread by a cough, a touch, or a hug, or sharing a glass, a couch, a sweater, people still act with prejudice.

GAY MEN ACT UP

Rather than sit back and wait while they and their friends died, some gay men continued to take things into their own hands and help one another fight this epidemic. In August 1981, when writer Larry Kramer appealed for action in the gay newspaper the *New York Native,* asking for donations to study the strange diseases killing gay men, he was accused by a reader of "emotionalism" and of claiming that "the wages of gay sex are death."

But others shared Kramer's concern. That month, a group of men meeting in Kramer's living room formed the first private AIDS action group, the Gay Men's Health Crisis (GMHC). Their civil rights struggle had taught gay men how to organize themselves and take action. Within ten months, although it had trouble getting any landlord to rent it office space to use for an AIDS organization, GMHC had a volunteer staff of three hundred and was training fifty new volunteers a week. By 1988 it was the largest private AIDS organization in the country. GMHC attempted both to raise research funding for the disease and to take care of people with AIDS. It began a Buddy Program, which matched each sick person with a buddy who would help him shop for groceries or clean his house or just be someone to talk to. GMHC also provided legal and financial advisers, trained everyone from doctors to family members in proper AIDS care, kept an eye on the quality of other programs for people with AIDS, and informed patients about the latest research on the disease.

In this spirit of activism, many AIDS patients decided they were not willing to wait for medical science to deliver a cure to them. They wanted to find any treatment that had any chance of working and give it a try. Faced with an incurable disease that no one fully understood, many were ready to risk everything. Before AIDS, medical science had come to a particular understanding of what sort of risks in treatments were worth taking. New drugs and treatments had to be very carefully and deliberately tested, first on animals and then on people who volunteered to be part of the experiments. These experiments, known as drug trials, could take years: ten years could pass from the time a drug was discov-

Because AIDS was first detected in male homosexuals in this country, the disease in women was initially overlooked, a discrepancy protested in this New York City bus shelter poster from 1990

ered until it was available for a patient to take. Certainly the young woman Hansen injected with leprosy would have been grateful if in her day testing was so carefully controlled. This was the point of this process, to protect the patient. Then along came AIDS, and AIDS patients said, we don't have ten years to wait, and we don't want to be so protected; we want to decide for ourselves if a drug is worth the risk.

Some AIDS patients found ways to get drugs that had been approved in other countries where testing regulations were not as strict. They formed organizations to get drugs from abroad and distribute them cooperatively. One such organization has carried everything from a German antidepressant derived from the herb St. John's wort to antibiotics not yet approved in the United States. Other patients, if they could afford to, made trips themselves to other countries for treatment, or smuggled drugs in across the border. Patients formed clubs to share information about treatments, meeting weekly with concerned and informed doctors and patients; they printed newsletters describing new therapies; and they created bulletin boards and news groups on the Internet. Marcus Conant began to hold monthly information sessions to which people from all over came to learn about the latest therapies.

But while these tactics might have gotten drugs for some people who were sick, activists were not content to sneak around the laws—they wanted to change them. In 1987 Larry Kramer formed another AIDS organization, the AIDS Coalition to Unleash Power, or ACT UP, specifically to fight for speedier drug trials. For its first demonstration, ACT UP chose a weekday morning march on New York City's Wall Street. The head of the Food and Drug Administration (FDA), the government organization that determines what drugs are safe enough for patients to take, was hung in effigy in front of Trinity Church.

In the fall of 1990, three years after ACT UP's birth, new guidelines specifically designed for AIDS drug testing were published in the *New England Journal of Medicine*. They were based upon changes advocated by ACT UP. The new guidelines called for as many people as possible to be able to try the drugs as soon as possible to see if they worked. To achieve this, the guidelines said, sick people should get a drug from the beginning, instead of first testing it on healthy volunteers. In addition, rather than trials being conducted only at research hospitals with small, carefully screened groups of people, large numbers of people should be able to try the drugs. Their own doctors should be able to prescribe them, and being different from the average AIDS patient—being female or Native American, for instance—should not keep anyone out of a trial.

These changes in drug trials were revolutionary in more ways than one: a new way to test drugs was created, and the design came not from doctors but from patients. Patients had shown that they did not have to wait for others to act, that they could take action to speed up drug research. Now it only remained to be seen if any research could outpace the disease.

For while these organizations fought for research dollars and speedier trials and struggled to care for their dying friends, more and more people came down with the disease. In March 1983 Kramer wrote in the *New York Native*: "If this article doesn't rouse you to anger, fury, rage, and action, gay men may have no future on this earth." In the nineteen months since his first appeal, he wrote, the number of people seriously ill with strange afflictions had risen from 120 to 1,112, the number dead from 30 to 418. The condition that caused these diseases had found a name, but despite the size and speed of the epidemic, AIDS was a name the President of the United States was not to mention for another four years. It appeared much of society still found this disease easy to overlook. But not Kramer, who ended his article with a list of the twenty people he had known who were now dead. And one more, he wrote, would be dead by the time the paper was printed.

AIDS WORLDWIDE

Although AIDS was first recognized in the United States, it took little time to see that people worldwide were infected. It appears that AIDS emerged in Africa before it began to show up in the United States. At the time, though, no one knew what it was. It was not until 1983, two years after AIDS had been officially recognized as a disease in the United States, that it was recognized by doctors in Africa. By 1994, although Africa south of the Sahara was home to only 10 percent of the world's population, more than two thirds of the people with AIDS worldwide were found there, and 90 percent of the cases of AIDS in women and children.

For reasons that are not completely understood, AIDS has a different face in Africa: AIDS did not appear first in male homosexuals and intravenous drug users but in male and female heterosexuals. One reason for this could be that Africans have high rates of sexually transmitted diseases that cause sores on the genitals, making it easier for the virus to pass between men and women. Another possibility is that the strain of virus that infects people in Africa is transmitted more easily between men and women. Long-distance truck drivers and migrant workers who frequented prostitutes while away from home certainly helped spread the disease from prostitutes who had a high risk of infection back to the men's wives in remote areas. In the end, AIDS affects three women for every five men in Africa, and as a result many children are also infected. If a woman who is infected gives birth to a child, the child has about a one-in-three chance of developing the infection. About 1.3 million children are infected

Road sign in downtown Nazareth, Ethiopia

with HIV in Africa. And because so many young men and women are dying of AIDS, experts estimate that by 1999 as many as five million children will have lost their parents to the disease.

At first many Africans responded to the new disease in much the same ways that many Americans did: they sought someone to blame. In Uganda, in a village near the Tanzanian border, it so happened that the first villagers to get sick were those who made their living smuggling goods across the border. As has occurred so many times throughout history, and in so many places in this epidemic, this led to a couple of hypotheses about what caused this disease. The first was that it was caused by foreigners, and the second that it was God punishing them for their illegal trade.

As had been true in the United States, people presumed the virus might choose certain people to infect. In the United States the first name given to AIDS was "Gay-Related Immuno-deficiency Disease." In Uganda, it was "robber's disease." When the disease began to affect people who had nothing to do with smuggling, it was given a new name, "slim disease," to describe how skinny people became. More and more people came down with "slim," until one out of every three adults in the Ugandan capital, Kampala, was infected. Along with that of Kigali, Rwanda, this was the worst rate of infection on the continent.

By the mid-1990s nowhere else in the world had AIDS struck with such force. In some cities, hospitals were overflowing, as were graveyards. People found themselves going to a funeral every week.

Most countries in Africa are poor: the average annual government expenditure on health care is $2.00 per person. People infected with HIV cannot get the care they need, develop AIDS more quickly, and survive less time with the disease.

Being poor also makes one more vulnerable to infection with many diseases, including HIV. One HIV-infected woman from Uganda described how patients in some Ugandan hospitals had to bring their own plastic gloves and hypodermic needles if they wanted to be certain that they were treated with sterile ones. The vast majority of patients could not afford these items. On these poor patients, ill-equipped hospitals would reuse needles and gloves, putting the patients at risk of infection.

Poor people may also find it hard to afford condoms or, if they use intravenous drugs, to afford clean needles. Or they simply may not have a chance to learn that they should use them. For instance, in India, where the AIDS epidemic is predicted to explode as we reach the year 2000, half of the country's nearly one billion people are illiterate, making it very difficult for them to learn about AIDS. Although India has developed very rapidly, the life expectancy rising from only 26.5 years in 1931 to 60.6 years in 1991, many of the changes brought about by economic growth are just the changes that increase the spread of the epidemic. As in Africa, the booming cities have drawn migrants who may patronize prostitutes while far from home. The same is true of truck drivers. Poverty and changing lifestyles have also infected India's blood supply. About 50 percent of the blood supplied to blood banks comes from people who sell their blood to make money. These are often desperate migrants from the countryside selling their blood to get by while they search for work. Unfortunately, this group has a high rate of HIV infection. To make matters worse, corruption and inefficiency have often prevented effective testing of the donated blood, resulting in HIV infection of blood recipients.

The World Health Organization estimates that by the year 2000 the number of new infections in Asia will surpass those in Africa. India alone, if current rates of transmission continue, will have five million infected persons—more people infected with HIV than in any other country in the world.

WHAT CAN WE DO ABOUT AIDS?

The suffering of people in Africa from AIDS reminds us of medieval stories of the plague: overflowing graveyards, endless funerals. But unlike the fourteenth-century Europeans, we are not helpless in the face of this plague. We may not yet be able to kill HIV, but we do know how to prevent HIV infection and how to treat people who are infected to help them fight off other diseases, and new treatments are giving people hope of a cure.

In July of 1996, at the annual International Conference on AIDS, held that year in Vancouver, one of the co-chairmen declared, "We are at a crossroads in the history of the pandemic. We are beginning to see glimmers of hope." For the first time in the history of the conference, the researchers who came together to present their findings were full of good news. Part of the good news was evidence that Thailand and Uganda, both hard hit by the disease, had reduced their infection rates. We have known for years that there are only a few ways that HIV can get from one body to another and that we can stop the virus in its tracks. Donated blood can be tested before it is added to the blood banked for sick people, preventing people from being infected if they need a blood transfusion. Using latex condoms can keep the virus from passing from one person to another during sexual intercourse. And using a fresh needle every time someone gets an injection keeps the virus from passing from person to person through the blood. The difficult problem was getting people to take these measures, known to prevent the disease. But now prevention programs are starting to bear fruit even in these AIDS-ridden areas. In Uganda, a 1995 study in the capital's suburbs found that the infection rate among new mothers had fallen from nearly 30 percent in 1993 to 16.8 percent. In another area, researchers found that while over 11 percent of men in their early twenties were infected with HIV in 1989, only 2.4 percent were infected in 1994. It is likely that mass public education campaigns and the unforgettable experience of watching mother, father, brother, sister, and friend die of AIDS have made people decide to restrict their sexual activity and to use condoms. One young Ugandan high-school student told a *New York Times* reporter that after watching his father die he would wait until marriage to have sex. He said, "My mother told me the way how my father got it. She advised me to take very much care and not to tamper with girls until I'm ready for marriage."

Other exciting research news has brought some scientists to consider an effective treatment within reach. AIDS patients who have taken a certain combination of drugs for a year have nearly undetectable levels of virus particles in their blood. The researchers are careful not to say that these patients are virus-free. It is possible that there are virus particles hiding somewhere where they cannot be counted. But it is clear that this combina-

During the 1990s subway and bus riders in New York City could read episodes in the romantic adventures of Marisol in this cartoon series, run in both English and Spanish, promoting safe sex

tion of drugs is able to do something no other drugs have been able to: it can kill HIV before the virus has the chance to become resistant.

HIV is especially adept at becoming resistant because it is such a sloppy reproducer. When any molecule that carries the genetic code is copied, occasionally a mistake is made, creating a mutant. HIV is such a sloppy copier a mistake occurs nearly every time. That means there are many mutant virus particles created, each possibly mutant in a way that makes it resistant to a drug. If a drug-resistant mutant strain arises in a patient who is on a drug, it will thrive, and the drug will have no effect on its growth. Such drug resistance can develop in a matter of weeks.

However, scientists have found that, given in combination with a couple of other drugs, a new type of drug called a protease inhibitor stops production of infectious particles. Fewer new viruses means fewer mutations, and three-drug treatment means any mutant strain would have to be able to outwit three different types of attacks at once. Hence HIV is killed before it can mutate.

Because only a handful of people who are taking the drugs have been studied by researchers, and they have taken the drugs for only a couple of years, it remains to be seen whether the drugs will continue to be effective, and, if they are, whether taking these powerful drugs for years and years will prove toxic for the patient as well as the virus. Nevertheless, why would such dramatic results offer only glimmers of hope?

In May of 1995 Marcus Conant started one of his patients on the then-experimental three-drug therapy. The patient, a man in his mid-thirties, had been HIV-infected for years but remained healthy. He had lived through the death of his lover from the disease. Then he began to develop the lesions of Kaposi's sarcoma. Before he began triple therapy, Dr. Conant found that the man had 200,000 virus particles per cubic centimeter of blood. One year later, not only had the number of virus particles in his blood dropped to zero but the purple lesions on his body had disappeared. For a year he had been taking drugs round the clock and living with the nausea sometimes caused by the protease inhibitor. Now, with no detectable virus, the patient and his doctor decided to risk stopping the protease inhibitor. Unfortunately, within weeks, not only had the patient's viral load zoomed back up to 100,000, but his KS lesions had begun to return. When he went back on the drug, luckily, the virus and the KS disappeared again.

This experiment taught a valuable but sobering lesson: merely causing the virus to disappear from the blood does not mean the disease is licked, and if the drug is stopped, the virus can return at an astonishingly rapid rate. This could have dire consequences. One of these tens of thousands of virus particles produced in the rapid burst of reproduction could be a mutant strain able to survive the attack of the protease inhibitor. When the patient returned to the drug, the mutant strain would not be killed, and the drug would soon no longer be effective.

This means that if a patient does not take his drugs for as few as three days, his HIV could become resistant. If a patient goes on vacation and forgets to bring enough drugs, or if he forgets to fill a prescription, and remembers over the weekend when the pharmacy is closed, or if he can't afford the drugs for a period of time, his life is in danger. And just taking these drugs correctly is no easy task. Here is the daily drug schedule of one person with AIDS on three-drug therapy and other routine treatments:

First thing in the morning: He takes his first doses of the three drugs, the protease inhibitor as well as two AIDS drugs of another type known as AZT and 3TC. The protease inhibitor is not supposed to be taken with a full meal, so he has a very light breakfast, just something to help his stomach handle his vitamin dose of a prenatal-formula multivitamin, plus the vitamins and minerals vitamin C, betacarotene, magnesium, selenium, vitamin B complex, and vitamin E. He also takes a steroid to fight the wasting away of muscle that can accompany AIDS.

At noon: He waits until lunch to take clarithromycin, an antibiotic to hold in check a mycobacterium carried by birds, because it might interfere with absorption of his AZT.

When it became clear in 1996 that new drug combinations were working, AIDS organizations had a new job: get the word out. This ad tries to reach both people who know they are infected with HIV and people who might be but have not been tested because they thought there was no hope of effective treatment

THESE WILL CHANGE YOUR LIFE

New treatments are changing the face of AIDS.

What have you heard about the new treatments for HIV? These treatments are responsible for vast improvements in the health of some individuals who take them. Many people living with HIV/AIDS are living longer and feeling better. Now more than ever it's important to get tested for HIV, and to get medical care if you're positive. For more information on testing call the AIDS Prevention Project at 296-4999.

Are these new medications affordable? Annual treatment costs can exceed $15,000. Most insurance programs will cover the majority of these costs, and Washington state will provide the drugs for free or at reduced cost for uninsured low-income residents. Call the AIDS/HIV Care Access Project at 284-9277 to find out more.

Is this a cure? These drugs have been able to radically reduce the virus in the blood and semen. While results are encouraging, we still can't eliminate HIV entirely from the body, and it can still be transmitted through unsafe sexual contact. For the latest information on new treatments for HIV, call Seattle Treatment Education Project at 329-4857.

Can everyone take them? Do some people experience side effects? Unfortunately about one in every three people find they can't tolerate these drugs. Even for those who can, the side effects, including diarrhea, nausea, and kidney stones, can be overwhelming. So while there's hope for some with HIV infection, it's still just as important as ever to stay uninfected.

AIDS IS CHANGING — FIND OUT HOW

Design by Stop the Torture

At 4 p.m.: He takes a second dose of protease inhibitor and AZT, along with the steroid and a dose of Bactrim, a drug that can fight a wide variety of infections.

With dinner: It is time for another dose of all the vitamins and minerals, except the selenium, and a second dose of the clarithromycin, again taken separately from his AZT.

At bedtime: His final dose of drugs for the day is a third dose of AZT, the protease inhibitor, and the steroid, along with a second dose of the 3TC.

Along with all of this, he occasionally inhales a nasal steroid to ease swollen and irritated mucous membranes that can lead to sinus infections, and when he remembers, he chews a medication to ward off the yeast infections of the mouth known as thrush.

How can he possibly keep all of this straight? Once a week, on Tuesday, he sorts his pills, using a pill box divided into four compartments for each of seven days. He has five doses, not four, and the compartments don't have quite enough room for all of his pills, and the protease inhibitor has to be stored separately with a chemical called silica to keep it dry, but with a few annex boxes he can make do.

Most people have trouble remembering to take four doses of antibiotic a day for the two weeks that they have a sore throat. To follow this AIDS treatment regimen, for years and years, is almost beyond human capacity.

More than that, the cost of the combination-treatment drugs is exorbitant. For most people with AIDS, the yearly cost of such a regimen, ranging from $12,000 to $20,000, is more money than they will ever see in their lives, much less spend on drugs for a year. This is perhaps the fact of the epidemic that most discourages researchers from having great hope: more and more, AIDS is becoming a disease that will most frequently attack the poor both around the world and in the United States. Within the United

States, more and more often the people becoming infected are people of color, and more and more often they are women. These are the very people who are most likely to be poor. By the year 2000 more than 90 percent of the thirty to forty million people in the world who are infected with HIV will live in countries that are poor.

In Africa, where the average amount of money spent on one person's health per year is so minuscule, $2.00, even at one hundredth of the cost the multidrug therapy would be too expensive. It seems very unlikely that anyone else would be able to pay for the therapy for the world's poor people: to treat the estimated eighteen million infected people living in poor countries with this drug regimen would cost $360 billion. A vaccine that could cheaply prevent HIV infection is the best hope for the developing world.

Fighting AIDS has been a tremendous struggle, not only with the virus but with our fears and prejudices. Through tremendous work, brave people have won for us hope in this fight, but the battle is not over. Fifteen years into the epidemic, nearly 23 million people are infected and 8,500 more become infected each day. We have a great struggle ahead of us. We can only hope that, knowing the problems that lie ahead, we can better prepare ourselves to face them.

OUR TIME OF PESTILENCE

In 1981, if a young man died in the United States, odds were he had had an accident, had been murdered, or had killed himself. Young people rarely died of infectious disease. And then came AIDS. By 1991 AIDS was the number one killer of men between the ages of twenty-five and forty-four in the United States.

In the wealthier countries of the world, we had begun to think we had conquered infectious disease. We had eradicated small-pox, ousted malaria, cleaned up cholera, tracked down and cured plague, overcome leprosy, and, we thought, beaten back tuberculosis. Not only that, with mass inoculation programs, we had squelched the battalions of childhood diseases—diphtheria, polio, measles, mumps, and whooping cough—that children of previous generations had to avoid or live through in order to reach adulthood. It all happened very quickly: my father's brother died of diphtheria, but I've never known anyone who had it; my older brothers and sisters had to live through measles and mumps, while I was vaccinated before I ever caught them, and probably so were you. In the past few years, some doctors began vaccinating against chicken pox, hoping to eliminate another itchy childhood rite of passage: your little brothers and sisters may not suffer the itchy bumps to gain immunity to this disease. For medicine, the twentieth century has been a heady time, in which it seemed we had, in part of the world anyway, found a way to overcome infectious disease. But given what we know about diseases, we should not be surprised to see plagues emerge among us again and again.

Many people have asked where AIDS came from. This is a difficult question to answer, and at this time, scientists can only guess, but it is likely that AIDS was not a brand-new virus when it began infecting people, but had probably been around for years, existing in some corner of the planet where it infected people so seldom that no one even noticed. Given how difficult it is to contract HIV, as it does not travel through the air or through the water, the virus needed very special circumstances to start an epidemic: it needed to reach people who were having sex with one another or sharing blood somehow in order for the disease to spread.

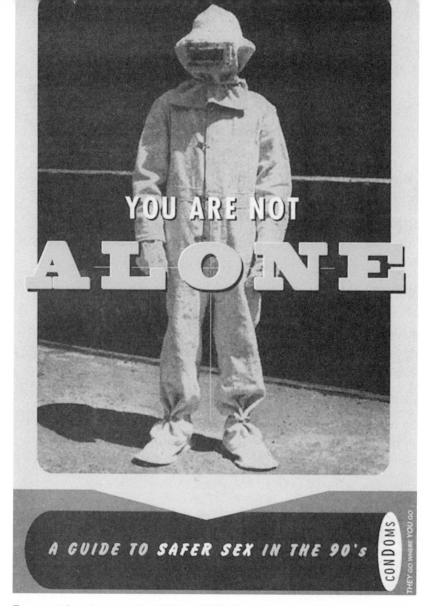

YOU ARE NOT ALONE

A GUIDE TO SAFER SEX IN THE 90's

CONDOMS
THEY GO WHERE YOU GO

For most American youth, AIDS and STD (sexually transmitted disease) education is now a routine part of sex education. As this pamphlet for young people on STDs points out, we are not alone—we must live with the microbes

Many viruses "emerge" like the AIDS virus; that is, they seem to suddenly appear just because they find a way to travel from person to person. Of all of these germs, however, none has spread throughout the world in the way that AIDS has. A hemorrhagic fever virus known as Ebola recently appeared in Africa. However,

Ebola is a virus that does not seem equipped to spread far and wide: it kills its victims so quickly they die before they can spread the disease.

Another hemorrhagic fever virus is currently raging through Central America and Asia. Dengue fever, which is carried by mosquitoes, is a tricky disease that is worse the second time around. If you have already been infected with the disease, you are more likely to develop a fatal form of the disease the next time you happen to catch it. Millions of new cases of this disease are reported annually.

Other viruses that have found a way to spread in recent years include a new hantavirus that emerged in New Mexico, Colorado, and Nevada in 1993, causing a rapidly progressive, often fatal, respiratory illness. Hantaviruses normally infect rodents, but when unusual conditions bring humans in closer contact with these animals, these viruses can spread to people. In the past fifty years, Junín and Machupo, both hemorrhagic fever viruses, emerged in South America because changes in agriculture brought humans into contact with infected rodents.

Although viruses have the most notorious ability to suddenly appear in epidemic form, they are not the only source of new epidemics: antibiotic-resistant bacteria are on the move as well. From the first time a tuberculosis patient was treated with antibiotics, scientists found that a drug would be effective for only so long before a group of bugs would develop that were not killed by the drug. Since that time, not only has drug-resistant tuberculosis emerged as a threat but many other organisms have emerged in drug-resistant forms.

What do these emerging viruses and resistant germs add up to? It appears that as it has been for thousands of years, so it will continue to be: we humans live on this planet with tiny creatures that live within us. Sometimes we become entangled in a battle for the life we share: at those times, if we don't take their lives first, they will take ours.

Over the centuries, in the course of these battles, we humans have learned all sorts of things about these bugs: we have found them out, in their tiny world, and then discovered the tricks they employ to become such successful killers. And they have helped us to discover much about ourselves as well, both about our bodies and our spirit.

In 1947 the French author Albert Camus published a novel entitled *The Plague* in which he described the plague coming to a town. His hero is a doctor who stays in the town to treat the victims. In the end, as the plague has finally left the city, Dr. Rieux pledges to write its story to share "what we learn in a time of pestilence: that there are more things to admire in men than to despise." Rieux listens to the jubilation in the streets celebrating the plague's passing with reserve, for he knows that "such joy is always imperiled." "The plague bacillus," he writes, "never dies or disappears for good . . . the day would come when, for the bane and the enlightening of men, it would rouse up its rats again and send them forth to die in a happy city."

Now you are nearly as wise as Dr. Rieux: you know that pestilence is never truly a thing of the past; and that disease can inspire unusual deeds, from burying men alive to sending off boatloads of orphans to dissecting one thousand mosquitoes to drinking horrible drinks. You are ready to live in a time of pestilence, to face the tricks the microbe world has to offer, and to discover what you can about the ways of the human spirit.

GLOSSARY

RECOMMENDED FURTHER READING

SELECTED BIBLIOGRAPHY

ILLUSTRATION CREDITS

INDEX

GLOSSARY

Antibiotic A drug derived from a microorganism and able to kill or inhibit the growth of another microorganism.

Anti-microbial A drug that kills or inhibits the growth of a micro-organism.

Bacillus (Plural: *bacilli*) A rod-shaped bacterium.

Bacteriology The study of bacteria.

Bacterium (Plural: *bacteria*) A simple, single-celled microorganism important in medicine because some bacteria cause disease.

Cell The smallest unit of life capable of independent function.

Contagious Able to pass from one life form to another by direct or indirect contact.

Dermatologist A medical doctor who specializes in treatment of the skin.

Disease A condition that interferes with the normal functioning of a living creature.

Endemic Constantly present in a particular people or country.

Epidemic Affecting many individuals within a region or population at the same time.

Epidemiology The study of the distribution and control of disease in a population.

Fungus (Plural: *fungi*) Any of a group of plantlike organisms that are either parasites or live on decaying matter.

Genes Molecules that contain the "blueprint" for an organism.

Genetic Having to do with the genes.

Germ A microorganism, particularly one that causes disease.

Immune Not susceptible to a disease.

Immune-compromised Having a disabled immune system.

Immune system An organization of cells and organs in a living creature that fights disease. The immune system patrols the body, screens for invaders, and attacks them.

Immunology The study of the immune system.

Infectious disease Disease caused by germs.

Inoculation Inserting a small amount of a substance derived from a germ into a body in order to arouse the immune system and so develop immunity to that germ.

Lesion An area of the body damaged by injury or disease.

Lymph node Immune system organ that acts as a filter for foreign materials.

Macrophage An immune system cell that eats foreign particles such as germs.

Miasma Invisible vapors incorrectly thought to cause disease.

Microbe A form of life too small to see with the naked eye.

Microbiology The study of microscopic forms of life.

Microorganism A form of life too small to see with the naked eye.

Mutant An organism differing from others in its species because of changes in its genes.

Organism A living being.

Pandemic A disease outbreak that is very widespread.

Parasite An organism that lives in or on another organism, which it uses to sustain itself.

Protozoa Single-celled organisms, some of which are parasites.

Pustule A small pus-filled bump on the skin.

Quarantine To keep separate in order to prevent the transmission of disease.

T cells Immune system cells (so called because they are processed by an organ called the thymus) that are responsible for particular defensive tasks, including fighting viruses.

Vaccination The name given to inoculation with the cowpox virus to provide immunity to smallpox that has also come to mean inoculation against any disease.

Vibrios A group of related bacteria, typically shaped like a comma or an "s," that includes the germ that causes cholera.

Virus A type of submicroscopic germ that cannot reproduce without infecting a living cell.

RECOMMENDED FURTHER READING

General

Camus, Albert. *The Plague.* New York: Modern Library, 1948.
> The story of Dr. Rieux, who one day discovers a dead rat in his apartment building and within a week finds himself in the middle of a plague.

De Kruif, Paul. *Microbe Hunters.* New York: Harcourt, Brace, 1926.
> If you would like to read more about the pursuits of Leeuwenhoek, Pasteur, Koch, and Ross, as well as other great microbe hunters, you will not find a more exciting account than this book. It is a classic.

Smallpox

Hopkins, Donald R. *Princes and Peasants.* Chicago: University of Chicago Press, 1983.
> This history of smallpox is thorough and entertaining. Hopkins gives a worldwide account of the disease by relating the history of smallpox in Europe, East Asia, India, Africa, and the Americas in separate sections.

Leprosy

Brand, Dr. Paul, with Philip Yancey. *Pain: The Gift Nobody Wants.* New York: HarperCollins, 1993.
> Dr. Paul Brand's struggle to investigate the secrets of leprosy is something like a detective story as he tries to understand this mysterious disease. This book also describes other strange disorders

that prevent one from feeling pain, and explains how the inability to feel pain is surprisingly deadly.

Stein, Stanley, with Lawrence G. Blochman. *Alone No Longer.* New York: Funk and Wagnalls, 1963.
This autobiography reads like a novel. Stanley Stein is an engaging hero, and his insider's account of life at Carville is fascinating.

Plague

Gregg, Charles T. *Plague!* New York: Charles Scribner's Sons, 1978.
This book tells the story of plague in the United States right up into the 1970s.

McNeill, William. *Plagues and Peoples.* Garden City, N.Y.: Doubleday, 1977.
A groundbreaking work on how disease has affected history. It is a challenging read.

Ziegler, Philip. *The Black Death.* New York: John Day Company, 1969.
The story of the pandemic that swept around the world in the fourteenth century is fascinating and gruesome. Ziegler gives a powerful account of the grim horror of the time and the helpless terror of the people who lived through it.

Tuberculosis

MacDonald, Betty. *The Plague and I.* Philadelphia: Lippincott, 1948.
You may not think that life in an American tuberculosis sanatorium in the 1930s would be a laughing matter, but Betty MacDonald manages to tell her story with a great sense of humor.

Ryan, Frank. *The Forgotten Plague.* New York: Little, Brown, 1993.
Frank Ryan gives an exciting account of the fight against tuberculosis and of the scientists who discovered the first antibiotics.

St. Pierre, Mark. *Madonna Swan: A Lakota Woman's Story.* Norman: University of Oklahoma Press, 1991.
Madonna Swan's story tells not only about life as a Lakota in the middle of the twentieth century but also about fighting tuberculosis and winning.

Malaria

Harrison, Gordon. *Mosquitoes, Malaria and Man.* New York: Dutton, 1978.
Harrison presents the fight against malaria as the exciting story

that it is, complete with photographs of the main characters. He begins with Laveran's identification of the parasite in 1880 and continues through eradication attempts into the 1970s.

Cholera

Rosenberg, Charles E. *The Cholera Years.* Chicago: University of Chicago Press, 1962.
Rosenberg has written a rich and engaging account of the cholera epidemics in New York City in the 1800s, with all the gruesome details of life in an overwhelmed and filthy city.

AIDS

Lucas, Ian. *Growing Up Positive: Stories from a Generation of Young People Affected by AIDS.* New York: Cassell, 1995.
In this book, young people talk about how AIDS has affected their lives.

Shilts, Randy. *And the Band Played On.* New York: Penguin, 1987.
No other history of the early days of AIDS can rival this book. The story of an emerging disease is told through an intimate account of the lives of the people who lived during this time.

Verghese, Abraham. *My Own Country.* New York: Simon and Schuster, 1994.
In 1985, when Abraham Verghese came to Johnson City, Tennessee, as a young doctor, people thought of AIDS as a big-city disease. In the next few years, however, Dr. Verghese was to care for eighty patients with AIDS in this town and learn firsthand of the prejudice patients fought along with their disease.

SELECTED BIBLIOGRAPHY

In researching this book I relied on many books, journals, magazines, and other sources. The following works were especially significant.

General

McNeill, William. *Plagues and Peoples.* New York: Doubleday, 1977.

Ryan, Kenneth J., ed. *Sherris Medical Microbiology,* 3rd ed. Norwalk, Conn.: Appleton and Lange, 1994.

Winslow, C.E.A. *Man and Epidemics.* Princeton: Princeton University Press, 1952.

Introduction

Bulloch, William. *The History of Bacteriology.* London: Oxford University Press, 1938.

Dobell, Clifford. *Antony van Leeuwenhoek and His "Little Animals."* New York: Russell and Russell, 1958.

Smallpox

Duffy, John. *Epidemics in Colonial America.* Baton Rouge: Louisiana State University Press, 1953.

Fenner, F., et al. *Smallpox and Its Eradication.* Geneva: World Health Organization, 1988.

Halsband, Robert. *The Life of Lady Mary Wortley Montagu.* Oxford: Clarendon Press, 1956.

Hopkins, Donald R. *Princes and Peasants.* Chicago: University of Chicago Press, 1983.

Montagu, Mary Wortley. *The Letters and Works of Lady Mary Wortley Montagu.* London: George Bell and Sons, 1887.

Winslow, Ola Elizabeth. *A Destroying Angel.* Boston: Houghton Mifflin, 1974.

Leprosy

Feeny, Patrick. *The Fight Against Leprosy.* London: Elek Books, 1964.

Hansen, Gerhard Armauer. *The Memories and Reflections of Dr. G. Armauer Hansen.* Wurzburg: German Leprosy Relief Association, 1976.

Richards, Peter. *The Medieval Leper and His Northern Heirs.* Cambridge, England: D. S. Brewer, 1977.

Stein, Stanley, with Lawrence G. Blochman. *Alone No Longer.* New York: Funk and Wagnalls, 1963.

Plague

Dols, Michael W. *The Black Death in the Middle East.* Princeton: Princeton University Press, 1977.

Gottfried, Robert S. *The Black Death.* New York: Free Press, 1983.

Gregg, Charles T. *Plague!* New York: Charles Scribner's Sons, 1978.

Hirst, L. Fabian. *The Conquest of Plague.* Oxford: Clarendon Press, 1953.

Nohl, Johannes. *The Black Death.* New York: Harper and Row, 1969.

Pollitzer, R. *Plague.* Geneva: World Health Organization, 1954.

Smith, Geddes. *Plague on Us.* New York: Commonwealth Fund, 1941.

Ziegler, Philip. *The Black Death.* New York: John Day, 1969.

Tuberculosis

Brock, Thomas D. *Robert Koch: A Life in Medicine and Bacteriology.* Madison, Wis.: Science Tech Publishers, 1988.

Dubos, René and Jean. *The White Plague.* Boston: Little, Brown, 1952.

Grmek, Mirko D. *Diseases in the Ancient Greek World.* Baltimore: Johns Hopkins University Press, 1989.

Keers, R. Y. *Pulmonary Tuberculosis: A Journey Down the Centuries.* London: Bailliere Tindall, 1978.

Kervran, Roger. *Laënnec: His Life and Times.* London: Pergamon Press, 1960.

Malaria

Bruce-Chwatt, L. J. "The History of Malaria from Prehistory to Eradication." In *Malaria*, Walther H. Wernsdorfer and Sir Ian McGregor, eds. New York: Churchill Livingstone, 1988.

Harrison, Gordon. *Mosquitoes, Malaria and Man.* New York: Dutton, 1978.

Jarcho, Saul. *Quinine's Predecessor.* Baltimore: Johns Hopkins University Press, 1993.

Institute of Medicine. *Malaria, Obstacles and Opportunities.* Washington, D.C.: National Academy Press, 1991.

Cholera

Barua, Dhiman. "The History of Cholera." In *Cholera*, Dhiman Barua and William Barrow, eds. Philadelphia: Saunders, 1974.

Chambers, J. S. *The Conquest of Cholera.* New York: Macmillan, 1938.

Duffy, John. *A History of Public Health in New York City.* New York: Russell Sage Foundation, 1968.

MacNamara, C. *A History of Asiatic Cholera.* London: Macmillan, 1876.

Pollitzer, R. *Cholera.* Geneva: World Health Organization, 1959.

Rosenberg, Charles E. *The Cholera Years.* Chicago: University of Chicago Press, 1962.

AIDS

Grmek, Mirko D. *History of AIDS.* Princeton: Princeton University Press, 1990.

San Francisco AIDS Oral History Series. *The AIDS Epidemic in San Francisco: The Medical Response, 1981–1984.* Berkeley: University of California Press, 1996.

Shilts, Randy. *And the Band Played On.* New York: Penguin, 1987.

ILLUSTRATION CREDITS

INDEX

Page references in italics indicate illustrations.